BEYOND THE WASTE LAND

BEYOND THE WASTE LAND: A STUDY OF THE AMERICAN NOVEL IN THE NINETEEN-SIXTIES

BY RAYMOND M. OLDERMAN

NEW HAVEN AND LONDON: YALE UNIVERSITY PRESS: 1972

041716

Originally published with assistance from
the Mary Cady Tew Memorial Fund.

Second printing, 1972.

Library of Congress catalog card number: 73-182210
International standard book number: 0-300-01543-7

Designed by Sally Sullivan
and set in Linotype Baskerville type.
Printed in the United States of America by
The Colonial Press Inc., Clinton, Massachusetts

Published in Great Britain, Europe, and Africa by
Yale University Press, Ltd., London.
Distributed in Canada by McGill-Queen's University Press, Montreal;
in Latin America by Kaiman & Polon, Inc., New York City;
in India by UBS Publishers' Distributors Pvt., Ltd., Delhi;
in Japan by John Weatherhill, Inc., Tokyo.

*Shakespeare and **T. S. Eliot** ruined us all.*

—"Confessions of Fausto Maijstral"

CONTENTS

PREFACE

To talk about the novel of the 1960s I have had to do some large-scale eliminating and some arrogant choosing —arrogant because the single basis for my original set of choices was simply the novels I liked best. Of my critical schema, I say what others have said before me, but I say it again since I am already guilty of arrogance, hoping I have honestly done what I say: I did not begin with a set of theories or themes, and when I did evolve a critical schema, I did not impose it on any work. In fact, there are more novels that "fit" the scheme than I could have room to discuss. I confess all this because I have taken the liberty of calling the subject of this single schema "the novel of the sixties." It is, however, only one direction among many that could be and have been discussed by critics of the contemporary novel. It does not, for example, encompass novels of social realism, protest, or reform; that would entail a separate direction, though the label "novel of the sixties" might apply equally well. Thus, my use of the term is a convenience only, and as such is only partially accurate.

My emphasis is on the vision and the form of this par-

ticular novel of the sixties, and I have often preserved
that emphasis by ignoring literary parallels. Certainly the
novel of the sixties is no more original than it can be;
what is said of it could sometimes be said of Dickens,
sometimes of Kafka, or Swift, or Melville, Hawthorne,
Dostoevski, Céline, and so on. I have spent little time in
claiming or disclaiming originality; I have instead concentrated on trying to discover the essential vision of
these particular writers writing at this particular time,
hoping also to reveal something of the American consciousness in the sixties.

I believe it is no longer cutting it too fine to talk about
the vision of a single decade. Writers more than ever
have become conscious of history and of the symbolic
value of turning points. Decades are treated with the
same sense of symbolic new directions as centuries have
been treated in the past. The year 1960, the beginning
of a new decade, contributed a great deal to the emotional drama and the new hope that surrounded John
Kennedy's election and presidency. The novel of the
1960s decidedly turns away from many sacred values of
the novel written in the 1950s; and nothing seems more
certain to me than that the novel of the 1970s will similarly turn from its predecessor.

In any case, I have attempted to isolate one set of characteristics, one configuration of themes, techniques, and
visions, which is peculiar in its combination and is the
basis of a new aesthetic and thematic response to the
ambiguities of human life. I am grateful to Professors
James Justus, Paul Strohm, Philip Appleman, Star Olderman, and particularly Terence Martin for intellectual
and practical assistance. Thanks also to Patricia Wood-
ruff, Manuscript Editor for the Yale University Press, for

her valuable aid in editing, and to Robert Merideth and Norman Holmes Pearson for their careful reading of the manuscript and their kind encouragement.

Miami University of Ohio R.M.O.
November 1971

INTRODUCTION: THE PROBLEM OF REALITY AND THE NEW RATIONALE FOR ROMANCE

The facts of contemporary experience are constantly beyond belief; calling those facts absurd does not seem to subdue them. There is always some small comfort in the neatness of categories, but only a glance at the day's headlines, a moment of listening to an advertisement or dealing with the clerk of some organization that holds you under the power of incredible inconvenience, and a jolting feeling that you have come unplugged or disconnected will destroy the safety that categories supply. The unbelievability of events is no longer reserved for large world affairs. We have moved beyond the enormities of Buchenwald and Auschwitz and Hiroshima to the experience of the fantastic within what should be the firm shape of everyday reality.

Fact and fiction constantly blur. In the past, science, assuring us that the unseen is unreal, sanctified *fact* as the basic unit of reality. If we were to build a sense of the ordinary, we had to build it out of fact. Writers had to write from fact. But the growth of mass society, the increased discoveries about the world of the unconscious,

and the supremacy of scientific relativism make us no
longer sure that our own idea of reality will be recognizable to anyone else. Indeed, if we glance back and
forth from the abyss of the unconscious to the daily passage of historical time, we can easily lose hold on the
whole idea of reality itself.

A tenuous hold on reality may not be unique to our
times, but the blurring of fact and fiction does pose a
problem for the contemporary novelist that demands a
new response. As Philip Roth, before *Portnoy's Complaint,* expressed it:

> The American writer in the middle of the 20th cen-
> tury has his hands full in trying to understand, and
> then describe, and then make *credible* much of the
> American reality. It stupefies, it sickens, it infuriates,
> and finally it is even a kind of embarrassment to one's
> own meager imagination. The actuality is continually
> outdoing our talents and the culture tosses up figures
> almost daily that are the envy of any novelist.[1]

To speak, then, of a blurred distinction between fact
and fiction, it is not necessary to trace the historical
breakdown in our sense of a firm reality to its scientific
or strictly phenomenological bases in the new discoveries
of physics or philosophy. What primarily affects Roth
and other novelists—and, consequently, what I am concerned with when I speak of a blurring of fact and fiction
—is how this blurring is manifested in actuality, in the
events, the people, the experiences and sensations of
everyday life, as we attempt to apprehend and make

1. "Writing American Fiction," *Commentary* 31 (Mar. 1961): 224.
A very similar comment runs throughout Joyce Carol Oates's novel
Expensive People.

sense of each day with just the naked eye and the vul-
nerable psyche.

While this blurring may not be new, it has lately increased in intensity as has our sense of impending disaster and our despair over a world with no apparent
meaning. The novelist of the 1960s has seized upon two
particular results of the blurring of fact and fiction in
order to help him discover a form suitable to the con-
tours of experience as he sees it: a growing sense of the
mystery of fact itself, and a loss of confidence in our own
power to effect change and to control events. Forced to
concentrate on fact for so long, we have come to see in it
a fabulous element and to suspect the existence of some
mystery behind its strange surfaces. The inability to comprehend or even wholeheartedly to believe in the existence of such a mystery leads us to a new kind of helplessness. We are bewildered by the "facts" thrown at us
from our own unconscious in the form of dreams and by
the growing unreality of ordinary life. The bewilder-
ment expresses itself in a fear that if we did penetrate the
mystery of fact we would find behind it some massive
unhuman force which has rendered us powerless. Either
because of us or despite us, power seems to reside in just
such an unknown monstrous force, and it manifests itself
daily through the mystery of fabulous fact. "No pollster's
survey," says Benjamin DeMott,

⨯

[is required to confirm that people everywhere, at all
levels of life, have made "satisfactory adjustments,"
have found ways of controlling the desperate awareness
of personal helplessness (by renaming it "maturity,"
"disinterestedness," or "sophistication"), have learned
to half-live with the most intolerable and deeply lodged

suspicion of the times: namely, *that events and indi-*
viduals are unreal, and that power to alter the course
of the age, of my life and your life, is actually vested
nowhere.[2]]

The point is that this mystery is no new Godhead—it
may provide us with a cause for the incredible element of
fact, but unlike God it provides no purpose for life. Our
response seems to narrow toward terror, rage, or atrophy.
Recall for a moment an image that, perhaps, launched us
into the 1960s: at the end of Edward Albee's *Who's*
Afraid of Virginia Woolf?, two people who have lived a
horrible night of indistinguishable fact and fiction culminating in "exorcism," the only possible act of love in
their world, huddle together and sing a song of terror at
something named virginia woolf—a something that is
surely closer to Walt Disney's fabulous cartoon wolf of
malice than it is to any woman novelist. The unreality
of a cartoon and the mythical voraciousness of the wolf
combine in an apt image of that unseen force with its
power "vested nowhere" that haunts us from behind the
facts of our daily life.

Because experience tumbles fact and fiction, fidelity to
some concept of "ordinary" experience seems close to
impossible. All ordinary experience recedes into the fabulous, and to speak of the ordinary is to do it like this:

Life was ordinary. He was going to step through some
door into a pitch-black room where suddenly the lights
would snap on. A thousand killers would be singing
"For He's a Jolly Good Fellow." His wife would be
there, his son. And at the instant that he started to

2. "Looking for Intelligence in Washington," *Hells and Benefits*
(New York: Basic Books, 1962), pp. 95–96 (DeMott's italics).

think: Today is my birthday—all the tenors, two hundred and seventy-five of them, would beat the shit out of him. They would cut out his son's heart and feed it to him, and he'd have to eat it—they'd have a way of making him. His wife would be doing a striptease under a magenta light. And all the king's horses and all the king's men couldn't put Feldman together again. He groaned.[3]

This passage contains much that is dominant in the vision of the sixties: the explosion of the ordinary by the fabulous; the protagonist's sense of helplessness even as he proceeds to a confrontation; the mystery of some *They* who have an irrational hold on things; and the ever-present tinge of the comic (black humor as it is called), almost as if the protagonist is compelled to play the clown. To contain this kind of vision and to respond to the fabulous nature of fact, the dominant pattern in the novel of the sixties continues the movement away from the realistic novel and toward a contemporary version of romance.

Many of the romance elements noticed by Henry James and Nathaniel Hawthorne, and posited by Richard Chase as the core of the American fictional tradition, continue to play a crucial part in the recent American novel. These elements are given a new vitality, however,

3. Stanley Elkin, *A Bad Man,* p. 120. Even the once sacred life of the businessman, guardian of the ordinary, has been invaded. The novelists of the sixties often make their mad protagonists operate in the world of business. It happens in *A Bad Man, A Singular Man* by J. P. Donleavy, *The Magic Christian* by Terry Southern, *The Moviegoer* by Walker Percy, and *God Bless You, Mr. Rosewater* by Kurt Vonnegut, Jr., among many others. We might also note that many critics who are concerned about the novel's "dying" or "living" seem to clamor for the ordinary in the novel. Novelists have largely ignored the clamor—perhaps we shall see that it is easier to ask for the ordinary than to locate it.

by the blurring of fact and fiction and the loss of confidence in recognizable "reality." While the novel of the sixties continues to render recognizable reality in less volume and detail of a certain kind than would a "realistic" novel, and while events follow upon each other without ostensible causation, our own confusions over fiction and reality give these romance devices a new relationship to actual experience. We can no longer say such devices present experience "unencumbered" by the facts of actuality. Indeed, part of the frightening impact of the recent novel is in the suggestion that its fantastic events may not just be capturing the truths of the human heart; they may be truly rendering the actual texture of human experience. The criteria of what is realistic in a novel must necessarily become shaky when we lose our confidence in recognizable fact. If reality has become surrealistic, what must fiction do to be realistic? What I am suggesting is that traditional devices of romance are now being employed as a way of capturing the absurdity of ordinary life. It is a radical response to a radical dilemma. As Ihab Hassan pointed out:

Forced beneath the surface, the hero in a mass society lacks some measure of definition, lacks the basis to distinguish between illusion and reality which the traditional novel afforded. It is this, rather than the absence of conflict between inner dream and public fact that prescribes the moral ambiguities of the recent novel and determines the involution of its form: the vague present or undated yesterdays of so many novels, their unworldly settings and symbolic actions, their submersed point of view, eccentric characters, and decorous structure.[4]

4. *Radical Innocence*, p. 107.

It is not just our recognition of the surreal unconscious that informs the dreamlike in recent fiction; it is also the recognition that experience itself may be a dream of another kind—"a dream of annihilation," as Thomas Pynchon describes it.

Nonetheless, we continue to recognize in the novel of the sixties two-dimensional characters, dominance of plot and action over character, and a continued hint of the mythic, allegorical, and symbolistic, among other such traditional devices of American romance. And there is one similarity which is particularly striking. Chase pointed out that the American novel is not interested in reconciliation, but that its dilemmas are resolved, or escaped, through a transcendent experience of horror, heroism, love, or death. The novel of the 1960s finds reconciliation almost irrelevant and certainly impossible. There is only one essential resolution, and it is not escape or even "accommodation";[5] it is the bare, necessary, and simple affirmation of life over death. We will see continually in the novels to be discussed that this affirmation is achieved time and again by transcending all questions of morality and social action, and transcending by means of some extreme experience which forces the protagonist to seize upon the very surface texture of life and affirm its value. This kind of transcendent resolution not only ties the novel of the sixties to tradition, but it also differentiates it from the dominant pattern of the fifties, when the Existential philosophy offered the primary mode for resolution.

5. In *After Alienation* Marcus Klein uses the term *accommodation* in explaining several novels written in the fifties. The term is very little different from what Hassan calls existential encounter and commitment. In any case, however helpful the term is for the books Klein does discuss, it is almost entirely irrelevant to the novel of the sixties.

There are two essential differences between romance in the novel of the sixties and traditional American romance. The first we have already touched on—the confused concept of reality motivated by a blurring of fact and fiction. The second is the controlling metaphor that attends the impulse to romance. "In narrative method the romance tends to employ metaphor as a structural device: while the novel can get along in its absence, the romance cannot do without the unifying use of metaphor." [6] Therefore, if the contemporary American novel continues to employ the devices of romance, it must also continue to employ some major controlling metaphor. In the past, critics have pointed out that American literature is informed with the metaphors of a "lost Eden," the "American Adam," and the "American Dream." We have repeated this assertion for so many years that we have stopped checking to see if it is still true of contemporary literature. It is not true of the novel of the sixties, which finds its controlling metaphor in the image of the waste land.

The contemporary writer is spurred by his reaction to a waste land world rather than inspired by his memory of a lost Eden, his expectation of a new Utopia, or his disillusionment by the betrayal of both. Novel after novel attempts somehow to catch an image of the modern world in some distinctive form of waste land that allows us to contemplate its landscape and learn some way to cope with it. For writers born in the years of the Depression, or raised in and under the shadow of World War II, the image of a promised land has lost its creative potential. Most of us are no longer bred on the kind of purely innocent hope that is destined to end in disillu-

6. Daniel Hoffman, *Form and Fable in American Fiction*, pp. 354–55.

sionment. We are an age weaned on tension and silent despair. Even before we are old enough to understand our environment, we absorb an atmosphere almost universally described as a dry and sterile waste, and if our imagination is captured by anything, it is the hope of moving beyond that waste land. This is the only kind of optimism we can afford; to start out caught in a waste land—like an insane asylum, a jail, or a dull state of deadened feeling, as so many recent novels do—and struggle toward overcoming that state is to construct a hope applicable to our particular times. Eden, Utopia, and the New Adam have no major significance in the novel of the sixties. If the memory of Eden and a related sense of loss continue to appear, they appear only as the universal remembrance of the eden of childhood—a memory as vital to William Wordsworth, to international modern psychology, and to the modern European novel as it is to American novels. As images haunting our imagination, these memories no longer connect to a sense of a lost America. If the promise of Utopia should continue to appear in the novel of the sixties, it exists as the universal hope for self-discovery. The old theme of the American Adam aspiring to move ever forward in time and space unencumbered by memory of guilt or reflection on human limitation is certainly unavailable to the guilt-ridden psyche of modern man. Undoubtedly distinctions by nationality have grown less and less valid in the modern novel. Perhaps the only things that distinguish the American novel as American are a particular quality in our guilt, a distinctive kind of laughter, and a home-grown fear of the superpower reserved only for residents of so powerful a superstate.

What is more likely to be the only distinguishing characteristic of the American novel is, as Richard Chase maintains, our continued use of romance. But because the old controlling metaphors have lost their vitality and distinctiveness, the imagination of the American writer, still working within the tradition of American romance, has turned to the image of the waste land. (We can see the beginning of this in F. Scott Fitzgerald's *The Great Gatsby,* for while no other American novel seems so heavily dependent on the image of the American dream, *The Great Gatsby* is the first novel to see the potential aptness of the image of the waste land for the novel of modern times.) It is an apt image, also, to embody those characteristics of the novel of the sixties mentioned earlier: the sense of mystery inspired by a blurring of the fabulous and the factual, and a feeling of powerlessness in the face of that mystery. And it is apt, in its mythical dimension, to Norman O. Brown's description of us in *Life Against Death* as all neurotic, all sick, all wounded in our vitality as if every one of us were a Fisher King. The image gives form to our worst fears—that the waste land which holds us in thrall could come from within us as well as from without. Most of all, it embodies the enduring wish of our age that someone, some quester, would heal us and make us whole. What I am proposing is not a plan for what would be proper in the novel of the sixties; it is a description of what does occur.

When I say that the image of the waste land dominates the novel of the sixties, I do not necessarily intend a statement of T. S. Eliot's influence on the contemporary novelist. Nor do I intend to match a series of novels against the mythical pattern of death and rebirth. My primary intention is to describe the world vision of the novelist of the sixties and how that vision has been embodied. What I have been calling the "image of the waste land" is meant to connote those characteristics of

The Waste Land (combining the metaphor of a wasted
land with the myth of the Fisher King and the Questing
Knight) which have intruded upon the modern consciousness and found expression in the contemporary novel.
In understanding the vision of the novel of the sixties, we
may sometimes find verbal echoes and direct parallels to
Eliot's poem or, in other cases, only a generalized use of
the metaphor of a wasted land or, in still other cases, an
implicit dependence on the myth of the Fisher King
cured by a Grail Knight bringing about the rebirth of
the land. The term *image of the waste land* is meant to
stand for the overall configuration of myth and metaphor
which can assist us as a critical tool in understanding the
dominant pattern of vision in the contemporary novel.

The characteristics of the waste land and the tenets of
the waste land myth are familiar enough to all of us to
have become clichés. (Fortunately, as we shall see, the
novelists of the sixties avoid cliché by means of radical
and violent juxtapositions and by their attempt to move
beyond the waste land rather than convert it to an easy
pose.) Although I will assume in future chapters that the
reader has some familiarity with Eliot's poem and with
the image of the waste land, it may not be out of order to
review some of the characteristics of the metaphor and
the myth that make up that image. In the waste land all
energies are inverted and result in death and destruction
instead of love, renewal, or fulfillment. Water, a symbol
of fertility in a normal land, is feared, for it causes death
by drowning instead of life and growth. Wastelanders
are characterized by enervating and neurotic pettiness,
physical and spiritual sterility and debilitation, an inability to love, yearning and fear-ridden desires. They are
sexually inadequate, divided by guilts, alienated, aimless,
bored, and rootless; they long for escape and for death.

They are immersed in mercantilism and materialism; their lives are vain, artificial, and pointless. Close to being inert, they are helpless in the face of a total disintegration of values. Life constantly leads to a reduction of all human dignity; the wastelander becomes idealless and hopeless as he falls prey to false prophets.

This picture includes characteristics of the modern world which, as I mentioned earlier, have entered into our consciousness and manifested themselves in our daily thinking and discussion. The myth of the waste land, briefly stated, revolves around the wounded figure of the Fisher King. He is the ruler of a land whose fertility and well-being are dependent on his health. A Grail Knight, a messiah figure, either by choice or by chance, seeks the Holy Grail and after a series of ordeals and temptations, culminating in a night vigil in the mad upside-down Chapel Perilous, heals the Fisher King (if he is successful) and brings rebirth to the land. To be successful the Grail Knight has to learn to give, to sympathize, and to control. Success is symbolized by the falling of the rain. The fish is identified with the Grail and is a symbol of "life-giving potency," just as the overall quest is an initiation into the mysteries of life and fertility. When we come to the discussions of the individual novels in the chapters ahead, we will be able to see how various authors use the image of the waste land in an attempt to comprehend and cope with the modern world. We will see, too, a continued demonstration of the use and alteration of elements from traditional American romance.

It would be ridiculous, of course, to assert that between 1959 and 1960 the nature of the modern world underwent vast change. The condition of the world as the novelist of the sixties sees it is very similar to what has been observed and written about since at least the end of World War II. The novelist of the sixties differs only in his response to that condition and in the particular form, mode, and metaphor he uses to express his vision. Ihab Hassan's *Radical Innocence* deals with the post-World War II novel up until approximately 1960; what he says about man's concept of himself and his world is still an excellent lead into the state of things in the sixties. Hassan tells us that the modern hero, to preserve his sanity, recoils within himself when he confronts the destructive element of experience and becomes either a rebel or a victim of the forces of society. His innocence is a radical refusal to accept the immitigable rule of reality and as a hero he emerges, just as the novel's form emerges, from a critical moment in his encounter with experience—the moment of initiation or defeat. Hassan summarizes the condition of the modern world and the hero within a pattern which he believes defines the structure of the post-World War II novel and which he calls "existential." Some of the characteristics of that pattern and vision are still pertinent: absurdity rules human actions; there are no accepted norms of feeling or conduct to which the hero may appeal; the hero is at odds with his environment and much of his energy is the energy of opposition; human motives are forever mixed—irony, contradiction, and ambiguity prevail; in a world of error even heroes do not possess complete knowledge. The ironic nature of man's world and a writer's fictional response ·

    isolate from the tragic situation the element of arbitrariness, the sense of isolation, the demonic vision; from comedy, it takes the unlawful or quixotic motive of the *picaro,* say, the savagery which is the other face

of play, as in saturnalia, and the grotesque scapegoat
rituals of comic expiation; and from Romance it adopts
the quest motif, turning it to a study of self-deception,
and the dream of wish-fulfillment, transforming it into
nightmare.[7]

We continue to live in a condition of fear and trembling,
and continue to recognize the dehumanizing and spiritually bankrupt nature of modern life. The response to
this condition, according to Hassan, is a series of variations on the philosophy of Existentialism.

I believe Hassan's description is accurate—particularly
about the novel of the 1950s. But Existentialism does not
explain what is central to the novel of the 1960s. It is
true that concepts like the absurd, affirmation of life in
the face of the void, commitment, and existential courage
still appear, but the novelist of the sixties does not depend on those elements for resolution—as does the
novelist whose vision is tied to the fifties, novelists like
Mailer, Malamud, Styron, Bellow, and Ellison. The
existential pattern is no longer employed as a source of
comfort, a guide toward coping with the world; elements
of that pattern, when they appear, are unorganized and
ununified in the novel of the sixties. There are other essential differences between the novelist's vision before
the sixties and his vision in those years. By pointing out
some of those differences we can discover more about
the distinctive vision of the sixties and provide some
generalizations that will be illustrated in the chapters
to come. We can also discover why certain authors who
have written in both the fifties and the sixties—authors
like Saul Bellow, Bernard Malamud, and William Styron
—are really just carrying the vision of the fifties into

7. Hassan, *Radical Innocence*, p. 121.

books published in the sixties. Even when these authors have used the image of the waste land, as in *Henderson the Rain King* or *The Natural,* they have done so with continuing fidelity to a somewhat existential vision. (It should therefore be apparent that the use of the waste land image is neither my sole nor my primary criterion for classifying a novel as a "novel of the sixties.")

There are almost no journeys in the novel of the sixties. Settings are stationary, and a massive static institution or background has taken the place of the journey as a symbol for the obstacles of human experience. When there is movement through space, as in Thomas Pynchon's *V.,* it is aimless, unproductive, uninstructive; Pynchon calls it "yo-yoing" and the image conveys the fruitless comings and goings of modern man as opposed to the possibilities of moral growth and spiritual progress that are usually symbolized by the journey. Even the quest of the Grail Knight is static, as in Ken Kesey's *One Flew over the Cuckoo's Nest* where there is decidedly a hero's quest, contained however in an insane asylum.

Similarly, the search for identity which has been so popular in recent years is muted in the novel of the sixties. The problem of individual identity continues to be of great importance, but there is very little of the deep agonizing introspection, toiling anguish, and long-suffering posture that have been vital to the search for identity even in novels as recent as Saul Bellow's *Herzog.* The hero in the sixties acts or thinks about acting; he spends no long hours in introspection, but pursues his identity haphazardly through conflict with nearly everything and everyone. Neither has the author in the sixties represented introspection by the old device of using several characters as simple symbols of different aspects of a central character's mind. Often, as in Kurt Vonnegut's books, the problem of identity is implicit but of very little importance; Vonnegut's real emphasis is on the nature of the world. Two-dimensional characterization is used specifically to prevent sympathetic identification with a character's tortured pursuit of a unified identity and to force us to focus on the author's attempt to understand the world as waste land. The use of character in many cases is reminiscent of the eighteenth-century English novel, where a character was known by his actions and the reader penetrated very little beyond the surface of those actions. In his "Afterword" to the Signet edition of *Roderick Random,* John Barth speaks of the surfaces of adventure and the spirit of the adventurous hero:

> There is evidence in some really recent novels, of a renaissance of this same spirit: hints of the possibility of a post-naturalistic, post-existentialist, post-psychological, post-antinovel novel in which the astonishing, the extravagant . . . the heroical—in sum, the adventurous—will come again and welcomely into its own.

Barth is right, for the form of the novel has changed again, and a new value has been placed on surface action. Most of the novels of the sixties use an omniscient narrator, and some avoid developing any one particular character as the center of the plot. Authors like Barth, Stanley Elkin, and Ishmael Reed often parody the search for identity, admitting the seriousness of the problem but mocking our deadly earnest overabsorption in identity seeking. Burlingame in Barth's *The Sot-Weed Factor* is one of many characters in the sixties who play upon the mysteries and possibilities of multiple identities—seeking as many facets of a single identity as there are roles for a man to play. A similar kind of character appears in Earl Rovit's *The Player King* and Stanley Elkin's *Boswell.*

They are characters like Ralph Ellison's B. P. Rinehart, except that they are used, especially by Barth and Elkin, as examples of an impossibly gigantic zest for life, whereas Ellison uses Rinehart to show those dangers of non-identity that are inevitable if one becomes protean and invisible. The novelist of the sixties seems to enjoy playing with comic book identities—with a mild-mannered reporter by day and a superman by night, with Plastic Man who can be anything, or Popeye who goes from schlemiel to muscleman on a can of spinach, or Captain Marvel transformed from a little crippled kid by the word *Shazam*. (These are cartoon characters actually evoked by Ken Kesey, Jay Neugeboren, Stanley Elkin, and others.) A cartoon version of identity provides the inevitable joke aimed at our sacred ideas of identity, but it also contains an intimation of secret yearnings toward the comic book hero's control over human events. As we saw earlier, the fear of losing power over our lives is one of the main preoccupations of the novel of the sixties, and it seems as if only a superman or Captain Marvel could hold control. The recent novelist has certainly not lost touch with the necessities of knowing oneself, but one decade's solemnities are the next decade's joke—and jokes in the novel of the sixties are very important.

In the novel of the fifties there was a widespread use of the mythic pattern of withdrawal and return—a pattern closely connected to American tradition, according to R. W. B. Lewis. Bellow's Henderson retreats from a world as actual as an aching tooth to the africa of his soul and then returns via NewFoundLand. Cass Kinsolving returns to America from the Europe of his retreat in Styron's *Set This House on Fire*. Even Ellison's narrator tells us in the "Epilogue" of *Invisible Man* that he is ready to return from his land of light bulbs, gin fizz, and

holy Louis Armstrong to the arena of human responsibility. The pattern is a variation on the one Joseph Campbell, in *The Hero with a Thousand Faces,* calls the
"monomyth." It is everywhere in the fifties and is particularly compatible with the existential vision. But in the
sixties we see little of it. If there has been a withdrawal
it has occurred before the novel begins, and in most cases
whether there has been a withdrawal is impossible to
determine. The blurring of fact and fiction with its resulting confusion over the nature of reality is so intense
that there is nothing very firm for a character to retreat
from or return to. Again, there is a static quality in the
novels; the hero, whether he is active or passive, is
trapped cold in a waste land where he can work for rebirth but hope only for a way to cope with the waste and
affirm that life is better than death.

Traditionally, of course, a character's return from
withdrawal is meant to symbolize his coming to terms
with reality, his affirmation of life in this world. In the
existential novel of the fifties, this is made a subject of
individual choice. But in the sixties man's power is reduced; he has no time to withdraw and ponder his decision; he must stay rooted in the waste land—in the
system that attempts to deny his vitality—and concentrate
all his energies on battling both himself and the mysterious powers that control him, thereby assuring himself
that he is alive. Both visions recognize the necessity to
affirm life and to simply *be* rather than *become,* but the
character in a novel of the sixties cannot and need not
retreat to a fabulous land to help make himself whole;
he exists in a fabulous land already and is constantly
assaulted by the fabulous nature of fact. If he wishes to
be whole, he can learn to give, sympathize, and control,
but even then he will only be able to say, along with the

novelist who has constructed him, "These fragments I have shored against my ruins."

Other corollaries to the Existential philosophy are de-emphasized in the novel of the sixties. The depiction of rebellion and victimization, proceeding through a pattern of saying NO to the destructive element of life and YES to life itself, is implicit in these novels, but it is taken for granted, as if we had already established that the pattern is necessary for human life. The traditional crisis of initiation into manhood appears primarily in the form of an initiation into the Grail mysteries—the mystery of affirming life—and the character who is initiated comes not from high youthful expectation, but from deadened weariness with the waste land. The hero in the existential novel wants nothing less than "the aboriginal freedom of man," as Hassan puts it. The novelist of the sixties views this quest for absolute freedom through an eye trained early by the sight of human limitation, conditioned by the atrocities of World War II and the fears of the Atomic Age. Freedom is a luxury in a world where survival demands a daily struggle. The current novelist has learned what Melville tried to teach all of us a long time ago—he has learned to lower his "conceit of attainable felicity." He is no longer obsessed with the desire to realize the American Dream of complete freedom, for he has recognized that the only thing man can comprehend and embrace is the mere texture of life itself—"the bed, the table, the saddle . . . ," as Melville saw it. Beyond that there are immense forces which render the land a waste and make freedom an irrelevant dream. Kurt Vonnegut's *God Bless You, Mr. Rosewater* offers a clear view of what is expressed in many of the novels we will examine: the necessities of coping with the waste land demand that man learn the small lessons of compassion and conscience. We could call it learning to care, or, as T. S. Eliot puts it, learning to give, sympathize, and control. It is a hero's task to give to others and to sympathize with them because the fabulous facts of experience make it so difficult for man to gain control even over his own life and to maintain a sane balance between pain, fear, and indifference. Thus, Thomas Pynchon tells us to "keep cool, but care"—almost the archetypal advice in the novel of the sixties. To seek "aboriginal freedom" is to lose balance, like Ahab, and willingly plunge into the ever-threatening abyss of solipsism. And to be Ahab in an age when we already fear that "events and individuals are unreal" is to be the man who nails down the coffin—a man shorn even of Ahab's tragic dignity.

One further distinction between the novel of the sixties and the novels just preceding it is a result of the continued movement away from conventional realism; and it has to do with the handling of sex. Although most writers stopped short of Henry Miller, just about everyone in the fifties presented sexual encounters with a reasonable amount of fidelity to detail. Even when sex was treated comically, it kept its details, its heavy breathing and fleshy fumbling, as in Bernard Malamud's *The Assistant* and *A New Life*. In the sixties sex too has become fabulous, another evidence of absurdity. John Barth's *Giles Goat-Boy* presents so many and such a variety of sexual encounters that it slips entirely over to the absurd, intending neither titillation nor "serious" mature man-woman love—or man-man love, or even man-goat love. Donald Barthelme's *Snow White* is about a heroine who has seven lovers (probably not dwarfs); she allows intercourse only while in the shower as the water pitter-patters on her back. When her lovers want to court her favors, they buy her a new shower curtain.

(Sex in the shower, incidentally, seems to be the rage. It appears in at least five novels.) There is a seduction scene in *The Crying of Lot 49* in which the woman has dressed herself in layers and layers of clothes so that it takes her seducer twenty minutes to undress her, during which time she takes a nap. In *A Bad Man* there is a wildly funny scene in which the hero, Feldman, tries to have intercourse with a wife he is not terribly attracted to. They take turns suggesting positions—on the color TV or standing on the bureau or sitting in a bureau drawer. Finally, Feldman learns something about his wife's activities that day which is totally irrelevant to sexual provocation, and he immediately laughs himself into an erection—something Henry Miller would deny is possible—continuing to laugh as his wife climbs on, and laughing so hard he wobbles himself right into an orgasm. The scene epitomizes the overall treatment of sex in the novel of the sixties.

Forced to encounter a vast confusion of fact and fiction, to deal with the horrors of a waste land and the constant imminence of death, and to seek power against a mystical force that may very well be an organized nothingness, the hero in the novel of the sixties has had to discover new modes of affirmation. In almost every case, as we shall see, no matter how affirmation is approached, its final achievement will always depend on some symbolic action that transcends tensions and moves the hero beyond the waste land—even if that action coincides with the moment of death or with some worldly defeat. (It is an action or gesture somewhat similar to the straightening of Cleopatra's crown just before her death in *Antony and Cleopatra*; the symbolic value and dignity of the gesture help her to transcend tensions of morality and the conflicts symbolized by Rome and Egypt.) The symbolic action functions as a pure affirmation of life, a gesture complete in itself. It is unlike social realism, where resolution must involve some plausible social response. Because the novelist of the sixties sees fact as fabulous, social realism has no basis for believability, and a single social response can never be plausible. On the other hand, the final affirmation in the novel of the sixties differs in one crucial respect from the final action, as Richard Chase sees it, in the traditional American romance—it does not fill the reader with a newly confirmed awareness that man has the power of universally significant moral action. That is too tall an order for a vision that only seeks some way to move beyond the waste land. What the affirmation does achieve is the small but valuable sense that life is simply better than death.

The post-World War II "existential" novel is a form of American romance defined by the individual's existential encounter with the facts of experience, and heavily dependent on the ironic mode. It pictures a world of chaos and accident where the individual constructs himself from his experience and from his confrontation with the agony of freedom. In the sixties the form of romance has veered toward the fable; it employs the mode of comedy known as black humor, and it is defined by the individual's encounter with a fabulous world—a world made a mystery by the extraordinary nature of fact, and made a waste land by an extraordinary sense of impotence. In the world of the sixties, chaos becomes insanity and there is no accident—all things are malevolently ordered either by the Institution or by widespread Conspiracy. The combination of the fable form with black humor, the waste land image, and the several themes arising from a blurring of fact and fiction create a specific configuration which is basic to the novel of the sixties.

Before proceeding to a discussion of the novels, it would be helpful to clarify what I mean by *fable* and by *black humor*. The modern fable is by no means a simple allegory. As Robert Scholes points out in *The Fabulators*, allegory is only one mode used by the contemporary fabulist. (Scholes calls the recent writer a "fabulator," and instead of fable Scholes uses the word "fabulation.") With the exception of Peter S. Beagle's lovely unicorn fable, the allegorical element in the sixties primarily reinforces the sense that contemporary fact is fabulous and may easily refer to *meanings* but never to any one simple *Meaning*. Allegory is often used to refer not to transcendental truth but to the invisible world of the unconscious or to the invisible world of mysterious powers that resemble conspiracy more than divinity. Thus, as Herbert Stencil hunts down the mysterious V. in Thomas Pynchon's novel *V.*, he runs into an incredible maze of possible meanings—all of them based on fact and all intimating some power beyond normal expectation. The route he takes is analogous to the route of allegory in the sixties; it points through fact to some fabulous power, but it points in a hundred directions at once.

The form of the fable is vital to our times; it is the perfect form for the two dominant characteristics of the novelist's vision—the confusion of fact and fiction and the fear of some mystery within fact itself that holds power over us. This is the modern rationale for the supernatural and for the unusual events that are supposed, according to definitions of literary terms, to characterize the fable. One of the things we constantly notice in these fables is that they are forever including some startlingly

familiar detail within their supposedly fabulous story—
the actual name of a celebrity, or a consumer product we
all use; a reference to familiar historical events; colloquial
expressions and colloquial fads; everything from an
actual nose operation explained in detail to a marriage
with the last remaining Medici. We are constantly
snapped back from an unfamiliar experience to the flat-
footedly familiar. Thus, the author not only creates a
wide scope for his novel but forces us to recognize that
any one part which appears fabulous may be as true as
that part we have recognized. Just when we are ready to
say Donald Barthelme's *Snow White* is a fantasy-game
playing upon the original fairy tale, we are confronted
with a court trial which results in the execution of one
of the modern "dwarfs" for tossing a six-pack of Miller's
High Life through the window of a Volkswagen. The
actual brand names jar us, as does the question of how
plausible the trial is—given the actual court trials we
have witnessed in the sixties. How do we designate what
is experience "unencumbered" and what is merely beyond our particular knowledge? How can we be sure that
the entire book is not practicing "fidelity to detail"? The
contemporary fabulist does not seek an escape to an unencumbered experience; he is attempting to deal with the
vital mysteries of contemporary fact. If we enter fully into
the spirit of the sixties, we will not only lose ourselves in
the paradoxes of fact, but we will begin to see the
strangely paradoxical possibility that fable, in a fabulous
world, may be "realism," for only through fable can we
be faithful to the strange details of contemporary life.

The most obvious characteristic of the contemporary
fable is its return to a self-conscious form that announces
itself as contrived. There is a regained joy in storytelling
and in the pleasures of manipulated form. Earlier in the

twentieth century, novelists tried all kinds of experiments with formlessness in fiction in order to capture the formlessness of human experience. Everyone from Joyce to Dos Passos sought new devices to make a form of formlessness. But in our current state of fear over the loss of distinctions between fact and fiction, the novelist asserts the artificiality of his fiction in blatant and extreme ways, thus demonstrating that fact and fiction have blurred and establishing that fact and fiction can be distinguished only through the radical use of fictional form. To stimulate an immediate recognition of the blurredness of fact and fiction, the novelist of the sixties has taken to inserting long mock-historical prefaces before the opening of the story, much as was done in the eighteenth century. They are supposed to assure us that the story we are about to read is "true" and compiled from actual documents. John Barth uses such a technique in *Giles Goat-Boy,* Thomas Berger in *Little Big Man,* Burt Blechman in *The Octopus Papers,* and Kurt Vonnegut in *Mother Night,* to name a few. But the writers leave no doubt in our minds that these facts, like all others, are as fabulous as the stories they support. The only thing that we can be sure is real is the author's contrivance. A great many novelists have taken to playing with the traditional legal disclaimer that there is "no resemblance to people living or dead." Attempting to demonstrate that we all may be as fictitious as the characters in the story, author after author mocks the disclaimer and shows how impossible it has become to make so definite a statement. Kurt Vonnegut tells us in the pages preceding *God Bless You, Mr. Rosewater*: "All persons, living and dead, are purely coincidental, and should not be construed."

The fable, then, is a contrived form; it is a form that reverses the trend of the "antinovel novel," as Barth puts it. It announces itself as fiction through a series of self-conscious devices in order to do what the novel has traditionally sought to do—bring some order and form to the chaos of human experience. While the subject of these novels reminds us that fact and fiction are blurred and that reality is hopelessly undefinable, the fable form paradoxically assures us through its radical contrivances that there is some difference between fact and fiction. It gives us some small sense of control, and in that sense lies some of the pleasure we get in reading these books, a pleasure which is often in tension with the pain the subject matter produces. Robert Scholes says the contemporary fable is more shapely and evocative, and delights in story for its own sake; it "joys us" and refreshes us as fables of old. It must certainly be the joy of control through form that he is talking about and not the particular vision of each book. For the contemporary fable, by containing the horrors of the waste land in a form that contradicts its content—a form we usually associate with happy endings—exorcises those horrors and implies the possibility of love and wonder in the world. But the joy it supplies is usually too complicated by pain to be very much more than fragments shored against our ruins.

Black humor as a term to describe the kind of comedy used in the fable of the sixties is as good as any other to explain a phenomenon difficult for most of us to comprehend. It is a kind of comedy that juxtaposes pain with laughter, fantastic fact with calmly inadequate reaction, and cruelty with tenderness. It requires a certain distance from the very despair it recognizes, and it seems to be able to take surprises, reversals, and outrages with a clown's shrug. Scholes has said it is closer to Swift and Voltaire than to anything in the twentieth century, except that it has none of the scorn, resignation, or hope of reform that accompanies satire. It is amoral and resists moral abstractions although it "exercises our consciences." It sees life not just as absurd but as a joke. That is why I say comprehending its spirit is difficult. It laughs, but the laugh is not a sunny one untouched by the incomparable miseries of man; it laughs where most of us sputter, write letters, talk about our friend the lawyer, or like Lear call down imprecations from the heavens. It is difficult to fathom how the black humorist can laugh, knowing what he knows. It is difficult to understand the Yippies of the late sixties, who laugh at Chicago even as they get clubbed, who tell us they will always carry tennis rackets (while they wear sandals, long hair, and the rest) so the fuzz will think they are part of the establishment—no one with a tennis racket could be all bad. Somehow they have learned to control, in their way, what frustrates and enrages the rest of us. Black humor has that quality of control in the face of the uncontrollable which is a traditional characteristic of comedy, but it is a control achieved through a quality of mind unique to people who have lived too long in a waste land and can only laugh to stay alive. It is a kind of neo-Jacobean tone, as Thomas Pynchon recognizes about himself and as he makes explicit in both *V.* and *The Crying of Lot 49.*

I recall seeing *Titus Andronicus* in Verona, Italy, during the summer of 1968; it was produced as an avant-garde absurdist drama. In the middle of the carnage of facile stabbings and lopped-off hands and tongues, Titus faced the heads of his two sons—rolled merrily onstage in a wheelbarrow—and he covered his mouth and giggled. It was the reaction of a black humorist; we will see it in Barth, Pynchon, Elkin, Vonnegut, and just about all the novelists of the sixties. It is a mode completely compatible with the fabulous world of the fable and, unlike the irony used in the fifties, it somehow transcends the absurdities it acknowledges without rancor, and makes possible an affirmation of life without the necessity of Meaning. As Scholes puts it—it does not teach, but it "humanizes" us.

Unlike Swift, for example, a black humorist can never deal from a superior position; he is always a part of his own subject matter. He must recognize the insanity that surrounds him, and he must recognize simultaneously his own contribution to that insanity; then he laughs to gain control over the pain of recognition, and to gain control over himself so that he will cease to contribute to the world's madness. The fear that we have lost control over our own lives, consequently, acts as a stimulus to black humor. While many social and literary critics feel that black humor is socially irresponsible because it lets us laugh at what most vitally concerns us, I believe black humor can be a social contribution as well as an aesthetic one. It helps train our perceptions to comprehend simultaneous concepts while we feel simultaneous emotions —we see the ugly insanity and the joke of a situation at the same instant, and we feel both the pain and the laughter. Both sides of the duality in our concepts and in our emotions must become linked and inseparable if black humor is to work. Joseph Heller give us comedy first in *Catch-22* and then he traps us for having laughed at what later turns ugly. The result is simple guilt, which is not as effective as the simultaneous pain and laughter evoked by the novels of the better black humorists— Pynchon, Elkin, Barth, and Vonnegut, who really "exercise our consciences," as Scholes puts it.

The older device of simply shocking a reader into awareness of his sins is unproductive—if social value and reform are to be criteria—because it only pushes us

deeper into a closed cycle: guilt—inaction—atrocity—
guilt . . . The ideal of black humor, therefore, is awareness *and* equilibrium; the actual social value lies in its
effect on both our awareness and our equilibrium—we
are not excused from pain or from our own contribution
to the world's insanity and yet we are not paralyzed by
our own perceptions—we are not made immobile like a
wastelander or like J. Alfred Prufrock. The combined
desire to gain control of our lives, to not hide from our
perceptions, and yet to avoid inaction has been, I believe,
the underlying impetus in the development of black
humor. Its greatest danger for the critic, however, lies in
its ability to laugh at the same thing it pictures seriously,
for as we try to explain and explicate the vision of the
black humorist we must constantly be nagged by the
suspicion that the whole thing is a put-on and the joke
is an elaborate web that suddenly disappears leaving us
as its only object.

In the chapters ahead we will see how the fable, black
humor, and the image of the waste land function together
to define the vision of the sixties. All the books discussed
contain elements of the fable, but I have arranged the
novels so that we can see a progression toward the pure
fable just as we have come to see our own world as progressively more fabulous. I will demonstrate, also, that
even the extreme form of the fable is not an escape or a
game with allegory—it is an attempt to confront contemporary experience. I have titled the last section of my
discussion "From Waste Land to Fable Land" not because it will signify our first arrival in the land of the
fable, but because it includes those novels that most
clearly use the form of the fable to move beyond the
waste land.

PART I: THE WASTE LAND AS INSTITUTION

The books discussed in Part I are run through with a growing confusion of fact and fiction, and a fear of something represented by the institution. The institution is a concrete image for those forces larger than us and beyond our knowledge that seem to have gained power over our lives. Because that image is concrete, the hero struggling to win back control from the institution knows what he is fighting and feels some confidence in his actions. Thus, the heroes in Part I are active; they are questers and Grail Knights. They are usually opposed by an authority figure who epitomizes the danger of the institution and the sterility of the waste land. In Part II—"The Waste Land as Conspiracy"—the force that rules us ceases to be symbolized by anything concrete; it becomes too vague, too ominous, and too enormous to be contained, and so it is called Conspiracy. This kind of abstract threat is more difficult to do battle with; its power seems everywhere and nowhere, and so the heroes in Part II are passive. If they become Grail Knights it is only by accident. There is no single authority figure to offer concrete opposition to the hero and help define the poles of his dilemma. The difference between symbolizing the mysterious powers that rule us by an institution and symbolizing them by a Conspiracy measures the growing sense of helplessness pictured by the novel of the sixties.

The institution, no matter what it may be, poses a particular threat in our age, since we have seen its power grow. At one time novels ended in institutions—marriage if it was a happy novel, an insane asylum if it was touched by despair; now they begin in the institution and aspire to go beyond. It is as if Holden Caulfield's quest in *The Catcher in the Rye*, ending in an insane asylum, signaled the end of American quests for the pure Utopia. Now the novel of the sixties begins where Holden left off—at the end of adolescence and in the waste land asylum, hoping to move beyond.

1: THE GRAIL KNIGHT ARRIVES

Randle Patrick McMurphy sweeps into the asylum waste
land of Ken Kesey's *One Flew over the Cuckoo's Nest*[1]
like April coming to T. S. Eliot's waste land: "mixing /
Memory and desire, stirring / Dull roots with spring
rain." He literally drags the unwilling asylum wastelanders out of the tranquillized fog that protects them—a fog
that is forever "snowing down cold and white all over"
(p. 7), where they try to hide "in forgetful snow, feeding / A little life with dried tubers." And, by dragging
them from their retreat, he cures the Fisher King, Chief
Bromden—a six-foot-eight giant from a tribe of "fish
Injuns," who is wounded, like all other wastelanders, in
his manhood. The cure takes hold most dramatically on
a fishing trip when McMurphy supplies the Chief and
eleven other disciples with drink for their thirst, a woman
for their desires, stimulation for their memories, and
some badly needed self-respect for their shriveled souls—
and all this despite the fact that the Chief "fears death by
water." ("Afraid I'd step in over my head and drown, be
sucked off down the drain and clean out to sea. I used

1. Page numbers for citations will be included parenthetically in
the text.

35

to be real brave around water when I was a kid." [p. 160]) The silent Chief's voice is restored and he becomes the prophet who narrates the tale, while the false prophet, the enemy, the Big Nurse, Madame Sosostris, who has the "movement of a tarot-card reader in a glass arcade case" (p. 188), is deprived of her voice in the last moments of the book.

The tale takes place in the ward of an insane asylum where an iron-minded, frost-hearted Nurse rules by means of one twentieth-century version of brutality—mental and spiritual debilitation. Her patients are hopeless "Chronics" and "Vegetables," or they are "Acutes" who do not, according to McMurphy, seem "any crazier than the average asshole on the street" (p. 63). McMurphy comes to the asylum from a prison work farm. He has been a logger, a war hero, a gambler, and generally a happy, heavily muscled, self-made drifter and tough guy. A contest develops between McMurphy (whose initials R. P. M. urge us to note his power) and the Big Nurse (whose name, Ratched, tips us off about her mechanical nature as well as her offensive function as a "ball-cutter"). The implications of the contest deepen; it becomes a battle pitting the individual against all those things that make up the modern waste land, for the Nurse represents singly what the institution and its rules really are. The drama of the battle is intense, and the action seesaws as McMurphy gradually discovers he must give his strength to others in order to pry loose the Big Nurse's hold on their manhood. As they gain in health, McMurphy weakens, and his ultimate victory over the Big Nurse is a mixed one. He is lobotomized, a "castration of the frontal lobes," but he gives his lifeblood to Chief Bromden who breaks free and leaves behind in the Nurse and the Institution not a destroyed power but a shrunken, silent, and temporarily short-circuited one. Beautifully structured, the novel provides us with both a brilliant version of our contemporary waste land and a successful Grail Knight, who frees the Fisher King and the human spirit for a single symbolic and transcendent moment of affirmation.

The world of this waste land is mechanically controlled from a central panel, as the narrator sees it, so that everything in it is run by tiny electrical wires or installed machinery. People are often robots or are made of electric tubing and wiring and springs, as the "adjusted" ones seem to be. The Big Nurse is only one agent of a "Combine" which rules all things including time and the heart and mind of man. *Combine,* as the word implies, is not just an organization; it is a mechanism, a machine that threshes and levels; its ends are Efficiency and Adjustment. According to Chief Bromden, the Combine had gone a long way in doing things to gain total control,

> things like, for example—a *train* stopping at a station and laying a string of full-grown men in mirrored suits and machine hats, laying them like a hatch of identical insects, half-life things coming pht-pht-pht out of the last car, then hooting its electric whistle and moving on down the spoiled land to deposit another hatch. [pp. 227–28]

Those are the adjusted ones. The ones who cannot adjust are sent to the asylum to have things installed so that the Combine can keep them in line.

> The ward is a factory for the Combine. It's for fixing up mistakes made in the neighborhoods and in the schools and the churches, the hospital is. When a completed product goes back out into society, all fixed up good as new, *better* than new sometimes, it brings joy

to the Big Nurse's heart; something that came in all
twisted different is now a functioning, adjusted com-
ponent, a credit to the whole outfit and a marvel to
behold. Watch him sliding across the land with a
welded grin, fitting into some nice little neighborhood.
[p. 38]

He is a "Dismissal," spiritually and morally empty, but
"happy" and adjusted. If you do not fit, you are a mal-
functioning machine—"machines with flaws inside that
can't be repaired, flaws born in, or flaws beat in over so
many years of the guy running head-on into solid things
that by the time the hospital found him he was bleeding
rust in some vacant lot" (p. 4). That is what is called a
"Chronic." Some people do escape in a way. People like
McMurphy who keep moving, and people like Pete Ban-
cini who are just too simple, are missed by the Combine,
and if they are lucky, they can get hidden and stay missed.
   All this is only the view of the narrator, a paranoid
Indian. But there is enough evidence in the way the
world around Chief Bromden runs to make his terms
more and more acceptable as the novel progresses. Among
the few characters on the "Outside" that Kesey takes the
time to describe is one of the insulting loafers who taunt
the patients while they wait to board their boat for the
fishing trip. The man is described as having "purple
under his eyes," the same kind of purple that appears
under the eyes of all the Ward's finished, lobotomized
products. There is, at least for a moment, a frightening
suggestion that the Combine's inmates may truly be
everywhere. For Chief Bromden it is no madman's logic
—after seeing the actual persecution of his father, family,
and tribe by the U.S. Department of Interior—to posit a

large central organization that seeks the doom of all things different.

The waste land of the asylum is characterized not only by mechanization and efficiency but by sterility, hopelessness, fear, and guilt. The inmates are aimless, alienated, and bored; they long for escape; they "can connect / Nothing with Nothing," not even picture puzzles; they are enervated and emasculated; their dignity is reduced to something less than human. Most of all, they are run as the Asylum is run—by women; it is a "Matriarchy," and behind almost every ruined man is a grasping, castrating female whose big bosom belies her sterility but reveals a smothering momism. So, McMurphy perceives almost immediately that Big Nurse Ratched is pecking at their "everlovin' balls." But the same has been true of Harding's wife, and Chief Bromden's mother, and Billy Bibbit's mother—and these are just about the only women you see in the novel, except a couple of sweet whores named Candy and Sandy. However, what is more startling about this terrible world is its leveling sense of order and its rules. In one incident McMurphy wants to brush his teeth before the proper teeth-brushing time. He is told that the toothpaste is locked up. After questioning the Aide about what possible harm anyone could do with a tube of toothpaste, he is advised that the toothpaste is locked up because it is the rules, and rules are rules. After all, what would happen if everyone just started brushing his teeth whenever he had a mind to. Kesey's point by this time is clear; the true madness, the real dry root of the waste land is not the patient's irrationality, but the deadly order, system, and rationality of the institution. What is normal is perverted and reason becomes madness, while some small hope for salvation lies in the nonrational if not the down-right irrational.

All of what the institution means and its effect on humanity come together in the single person of the Big Nurse, who causes the patients' hopelessness, their inadequacy, fear, anxiety, and alienation. She is the institution itself, the waste land personified. White and starched stiff, she suggests Melville's plunge into the dreadful ambiguity and possible evil that could live in the heart of what is white. (McMurphy wears fancy shorts with white jumping whales on them, given to him by an Oregon State co-ed who called him a "symbol.") But with the Big Nurse the ambiguity is only superficial and thrives only on the name of respectability—her real villainy is clear. She is the enemy, the "Belladonna," obstacle to the Grail Knight. She enervates her patients by playing upon their fears, guilts, and inadequacies. She and all other castrators are "people who try to make you weak so they can get you to toe the line, to follow their rules, to live like they want you to. And the best way to do this, to get you to knuckle under, is to weaken you by gettin' you where it hurts the worst" (p. 58). She is relentless in her crippling pity and capable of using any weapon in order to preserve her control. She has handpicked her aides, three shadowy and sadistic black men who are hooked to her by electrical impulses of hate. They have been twisted by white brutality, and their response is savage. As weapons in the Big Nurse's arsenal, they serve as symbols of the force of guilt which she uses to torment her patients. Guilt and the black man twine identities in the white mind to cut deeper into its already vitiated self-respect.

The Big Nurse is continually pictured in images of frost or machinery, or as a crouching swelling beast. She is described as a collection of inert materials, plastic, porcelain—any of modern America's favorite respectable synthetics. "Her face is smooth, calculated, and precision-made, like an expensive baby doll, skin like flesh-colored enamel, blend of white and cream and baby-blue eyes, small nose, pink little nostrils—everything working together except the color on her lips and fingernails, and the size of her bosom" (p. 5). She is sexless and cold enough to halt McMurphy's lecture on how a man can always win out over a woman; she is "impregnable" in almost every sense, even by so vaunted a "whambam" as McMurphy.

> What she dreams of there in the center of those wires is a world of precision efficiency and tidiness like a pocket watch with a glass back, a place where the schedule is unbreakable and all the patients who aren't Outside, obedient under her beam, are wheelchair Chronics with catheter tubes run direct from every pant-leg to the sewer under the floor. [p. 27]

She controls clock time, has all the rules on her side, and uses insinuation like a torture rack. Fear, cowardice, and timidity are all she sees in man. She sums up all that is debilitating to the individual about a modern world of massive institutions. In waste land terms, she is the keeper of the keys, the false prophet; for not only is she the cause of enervation and division, but she also perverts the holy words that are the key to coping with the waste land. When she gives she emasculates; when she sympathizes she reduces; and when she controls she destroys. McMurphy, the Grail Knight, the savior, not only must contest her power, but must listen to, learn how to live by, and restore the true meaning of the holy words from "What the Thunder Said": Give, Sympathize, Control.

The narrative movement of the novel is built around McMurphy's growth in knowledge and his progress toward curing Chief Bromden. As he learns to give and to sympathize, he moves toward death while the Chief moves toward rebirth, "blown-up" to full size by Mc-Murphy's sacrifice and gift of self-control. At the beginning we are given two images foreshadowing McMurphy's fate: Ellis, the patient who stands like an empty Christ, arms outstretched in tortured crucifixion, fixed that way by an electric shock machine used as a weapon of the institution; and Ruckly, blanked of all but mindless, obscene answers and beaten by the trump card of the institution—lobotomy—beaten as a means of dealing with his rebellion. McMurphy will also be personally beaten, crucified, and lobotomized because there is no final victory over the Big Nurse and her waste land; she will continue just as Eliot's waste land continues after the rain that falls.

> She's too big to be beaten. She covers one whole side of the room like a Jap statue. There's no moving her and no help against her. She's lost a little battle here today, but it's a minor battle in a big war that she's been winning and that she'll go on winning . . . just like the Combine, because she has all the power of the Combine behind her. [p. 109]

But the little battle she loses is enough to cure the Chief and bring a little rain to a parched land.

Ironically, McMurphy enters the asylum supposedly on a request for "transfer" to get "new blood" for his poker games, but from that very entrance, as he laughs, winks, and goes around shaking limp hands, it is he that does the transferring and the giving of blood. The first foretelling of his effect on Chief Bromden comes as

McMurphy seizes the Chief's hand: "That palm made a scuffing sound against my hand. I remember the fingers were thick and strong closing over mine, and my hand commenced to feel peculiar and went to swelling up out there on my stick of an arm, like he was transmitting his own blood into it. It rang with blood and power. It blowed up near as big as his" (pp. 23–24). He brings contact, the human touch, to a place sterilized of all but inverted relationships. His giving and his sacrifice are not, however, a continuous unbroken process, but are correlated to his learning. He launches into full battle with the Big Nurse and begins pulling the patients out of their tranquillized fog. His first assault reaches its peak in the contest over TV privileges.

McMurphy strengthens the other men enough to rebel in unison against the Big Nurse, and he does it by the symbolic gesture of attempting to lift a massive "control panel." It is a symbol of his resistance and willingness to keep trying even when he is going to be beaten, even when he *knows* he is going to be beaten. The strain on him is balanced by his effect on the men and on Chief Bromden in particular. The Chief asserts himself for the first time. He raises his hand to join the vote against the Big Nurse and recognizes that no external power is controlling him—he himself had lifted his own arm expressing his own decision. This first sign of self-control, inspired by McMurphy's struggle with the control panel, leads the Chief out of his fog and out of his safety; he ceases to be the blind, impotent Tiresias and literally begins to see again. Waking up late at night, he looks out a window and sees clearly, without hallucination— something he has been unable to do since he has been in the asylum. What he sees, on another level, is that McMurphy has succeeded in being himself, that it is possible to be yourself without hiding and without the Combine getting you. But just as the Chief makes this discovery McMurphy learns what it really means to be "committed" in this asylum, and he faces the temptation that is hazard to any Grail Knight—the temptation to quit.

Learning that most of the patients are "voluntary," that he is one of the few "committed," and that the duration of his commitment is to be determined by the Big Nurse, McMurphy becomes "cagey" (an ominous word in this mechanized world). He promptly ceases giving and he ceases sympathizing. The immediate result is an assertion of the waste land—Cheswick, one of the patients dependent on McMurphy, drowns himself. Without resistance from the Grail Knight, the waste land perverts water, the symbol of fertility, into the medium of death.

But the demands made on McMurphy by the weaker inmates determine his return to battle, for the weak are driven to the waste land by "Guilt. Shame. Fear. Self-belittlement," while the strong are driven by the needs of the weak. As the Chief ultimately realizes, McMurphy is driven by the inmates, and this drive "had been making him go on for weeks, keeping him standing long after his feet and legs had given out, weeks of making him wink and grin and laugh and go on with his act long after his humor had been parched dry between two electrodes" (pp. 304–05). To signal his renewed challenge to the institution and his acceptance of commitment, McMurphy stands up at what looks like the Big Nurse's decisive victory, strides mightily across the ward, "the iron in his boot heels cracking lightning out of the tile," and runs his fist through the Big Nurse's enormous glass window, shattering her dry hold as "the glass comes apart

like water splashing." McMurphy knows where his gesture will lead; he was told in the very beginning that
making trouble and "breaking windows" and all like
that will lead him to crucifixion on the shock table and
destruction by lobotomy.

What McMurphy has learned is the secret of "What
the Thunder Said," for, as one critic of Eliot's poem explained it,

> If we can learn to give of ourselves and to live in sym-
> pathetic identification with others, perhaps we may
> also learn the art of self-control and thereby prepare
> ourselves to take on the most difficult of responsibili-
> ties: that of giving directions ourselves, of controlling
> our destinies and perhaps those of others, as an expert
> helmsman controls a ship.[2]

McMurphy as helmsman leads his twelve followers, including Chief Bromden, aboard a ship and on to a fishing trip where, through his active sympathy, he gives
them the gift of life so that they may gain control of
their own destinies. The fishing trip—considering the
fish as the traditional mystical symbol of fertility—is the
central incident in McMurphy's challenge to the waste
land. What he gives to the men is drained from his own
lifeblood, and the path of his descent to weariness is
crossed by Chief Bromden "pumped up" to full size, the
cured Fisher King. And at that point, we are told "the
wind was blowing a few drops of rain." "*Damyata*:
The boat responded / Gaily, to the hand expert with sail
and oar."

McMurphy gives the men not only self-confidence and
a renewed sense of virility, but also what Kesey sees as

---

2. Kimon Friar and John Malcolm Brinin, eds., *Modern Poetry*
(New York: Appleton-Century-Crofts, 1951), p. 472.

man's only weapon against the waste land—laughter. There has been no laughter in the asylum; McMurphy notices that immediately and comments, "when you lose your laugh you lose your *footing.*" By the end of the fishing trip McMurphy has everyone laughing "because he knows you have to laugh at the things that hurt you just to keep yourself in balance, just to keep the world from running you plumb crazy" (pp. 237–38). In effect, he teaches the men to be black humorists, and it is the vision and the balance of black humor that Kesey attempts to employ as a stay against the waste land. To Kesey, being human and having control means being able to laugh, for the rational ordered world has done us in, and only an insurgence of energy from the irrational can break through the fear and sterility that have, paradoxically, made the world go mad. It is ultimately their laughter that the men cram down the Big Nurse's maw in their brief moment of victory.

In the final section of the book, McMurphy works with growing fatigue and resignation toward his inevitable sacrifice. He battles with the Nurse's Aides, gets repeated shock treatments, has a chance to capitulate to the Big Nurse and refuses, returns from the cruelty of the shock table to the ward where he is faced with the charge of mixed and ulterior motives, and finally holds his mad vigil in the upside-down world of the Chapel Perilous. But madness here is antiorder, and so a sign of health. The scene is the night of Billy Bibbit's lost virginity. McMurphy and his followers run wild, completely subverting the order of the Big Nurse's ward and violating the sanctity of all rules. Billy's entrance into manhood symbolizes their initiation into the final mysteries of life and fertility. All this is as it should be during and following a vigil in the Chapel Perilous. But, as we already know, you cannot beat the Big Nurse. She regains her power by cowing Billy with shame and forcing him to betray his deliverer. Billy, broken again, slits his throat, and the Big Nurse attempts one last time to turn guilt against McMurphy. His response is the ultimate sacrificial gesture; he rips open her dress, exposing her mountainous and smothering breasts, and chokes her—not able to kill her, but only to weaken and silence her. The contest ends in violence, the individual's last offense against the immensities that oppress him. Kesey, like John Hawkes, finds something ultimately necessary and cleansing about violence.

At McMurphy's fall "he gave a cry. At the last, falling backward, his face appearing to us for a second upside down before he was smothered on the floor by a pile of white uniforms, he let himself cry out: A sound of cornered-animal fear and hate and surrender and defiance" (p. 305). It was the only sound and the only sign that "he might be anything other than a sane willful, dogged man performing a hard duty." His madness is all the salvation the twentieth century can muster, for to give and to sympathize in our kind of waste land is itself a sign of madness. McMurphy is lobotomized, and in the final moments of the book Chief Bromden snuffs out the life of the body connected to that already dead spirit, and with his gift of life, seizes the huge "control panel" McMurphy had blown him up to lift, and spins it through the asylum window. "The glass splashed out in the moon, like a bright cold water baptizing the sleeping earth" (p. 310). The Fisher King is free. Although the waste land remains, McMurphy the readheaded Grail Knight has symbolically transcended it through his gesture of sacrifice, and at least allowed others to "Come in under the shadow of this red rock."

One Flew over the Cuckoo's Nest is a modern fable pitting a fabulous kind of good against a fabulous kind of evil and making use of many of the traditional devices of American romance which were mentioned in the Introduction. For example: it emphasizes plot and action (not character), and it employs myth, allegory, and symbol. There are equally obvious points of contact between the themes of this book and traditional American themes: for example, the rebellion against old orders and old hierarchies, and the need for communal effort in the face of an alien and overwhelmingly negative force. This book is more closely tied to American tradition than any other book we will deal with, and yet there is much in it that offers a paradigm for what is different about the characteristic vision in the American novel of the 1960s. It does not return to the past, gaze toward the future, or travel to the unknown to get its "romance" setting. The setting is the static institution which sums up both the preoccupation of our age with the mystery of power, and the substitution of an image of the waste land for the image of a journey between Eden and Utopia. It is shot through with the vitality of its use of the here and the now. We are constantly shocked into discovering how the book is really tied to the recognizable, not to the distant or strange, but to our very own—to technology we know of, to clichés we use, to an atmosphere possible only in the atomic tension of our times. Just as no one can confidently say who is mad and who is not in Kesey's novel, no one can say in what sense his story is real and in what sense it is fiction. The narrator sounds a note that echoes everywhere in the sixties: "You think this is too horrible to have really happened, this is too awful to be the truth! But, please. It's still hard for me to have a clear mind thinking on it. But it's the truth even if it didn't happen" (p. 8). The romance elements in the book are not based on devices that whisk us away to some "theatre, a little removed from the highway of ordinary travel," [3] and then whisk us back fueled up with truth. We suspect with horror that what we are seeing very possibly *is* our highway of ordinary travel, fantastic as it may seem.

The romance elements in *One Flew over the Cuckoo's Nest* are inspired by a world vision which questions the sanity of fact. It is a cartoon and comic-strip world—where a man's muscles can be "blown-up" like Popeye's arms after a taste of spinach—"a cartoon world, where the figures are flat and outlined in black, jerking through some kind of goofy story that might be real funny if it weren't for the cartoon figures being real guys" (p. 31). Not only is this a good image of Kesey's world, but it supplies the pattern for his character development. The movement from being a cartoon figure to becoming a painfully real guy is exemplified by Billy Bibbit. His name and his personality are reminiscent of comic-strip character Billy Batson, a little crippled kid, weak and helpless, who could say "Shazam" and turn into Captain Marvel. And just when Billy Bibbit stops being a little crippled kid, after the comic book fun of his tumble with Candy, just when his "whambam" Shazam should turn him into this big, powerful, unbeatable Captain Marvel, the Big Nurse turns him into a real guy—a judas, in fact, who proceeds from betrayal to slitting his very real throat.[4] While Kesey attempts to employ the mode of black humor, and while he does see the value of laughter

3. Nathaniel Hawthorne, "Preface" to *Blithedale Romance* (New York: Norton, 1958), p. 27.

4. Kesey actually refers directly to the "Captain Marvel" comic strip in a long discussion in his second novel *Sometimes a Great Notion*, pp. 142–43.

in coping with the waste land, one suspects that he is more pained and bittered by the "real guy" than a black humorist can afford to be. His humor often loses that fine edge between pain and laughter that we see in Elkin, Vonnegut, Barth, and Pynchon, while his "flat" portrayal of women and of Blacks is more stereotypic and uncomfortable than funny or fitting with his cartoon character pattern. It borders too much on the simplistic.

The romance elements also revolve around our new version of mystery. Though we may certainly be tempted to call it paranoia, it is definitely a part of the equipment of our times, and it is undoubtedly malevolent. The Big Nurse, The Combine, The Asylum—all three seem to symbolize that immense power that reduces us, and that seems to be mysteriously unlocatable. Kesey is one of those writers of the sixties who explore some mystery about Fact itself that portends mostly defeat for man. This sense of mystery adds complexity to the paradoxes of what is mad and sane, real and unreal, for it drives us to seek its heart in some huge force conspiring against us. Although it arises in connection with the image of the waste land, this mystery is the antipathy of Eliot's hoped-for God. It is only a further cause of divisive fear.

The mystery is best represented, to Kesey, by the asylum itself, but he leaves us with two possible locations of the mystery's source. It could be located somewhere external to us as Chief Bromden sees it, or as McMurphy tries to explain, maybe blaming it on a Combine is "just passing the buck." It may really be our own "deep-down hang-up that's causing the gripes." Perhaps there is some big bad wolf—and then perhaps there is only us. In the past the essential shock in American fictional experience has been a character's discovery that deep down he too is capable of evil; the shock in the sixties is the character's discovery that deep down he may be a source of unrelenting insanity. Down there, perhaps, that unknowable and seemingly immense power against us comes into being and then mounts to become a world gone mad. Against that or within that the writer, the prophet, sees new paradoxes of reason and irrationality, fact and mystery, and writes his novels no longer sure of what is fact or fiction and where malevolence lies—within or without. His only rationale can be the one stated by one of Kesey's characters: "These things don't happen. . . . These things are fantasies you lie awake at night dreaming up and then are afraid to tell your analyst. You're not *really* here. That wine isn't real; *none* of this exists. Now, let's go on from there" (p. 285).

2: THE FISHER KING TURNS WARDEN

In Ken Kesey's upside-down world, there remains a toe-hold for McMurphy's sturdy boot; even though inverted, good is still distinguishable from evil. The Big Nurse and the institution may appear to be defenders of the good, but we have no trouble seeing that their version of goodness and sanity is the real enemy. McMurphy's motives may sometimes be doubted but we have no real problem seeing his true virtue. His sacrifice gives us, through our recognition of a difference between good and evil, a renewed belief that there is something recognizable about reality, something ordinary which will help us recover a sense that fact and fiction are distinguishable.

But renewal is harder to come by in most novels of the sixties than it is in *One Flew over the Cuckoo's Nest*. In most there is not only a sense that the world is an inverted mad waste land where only radical and violent responses can prove a man's humanity, but also an intensified fear that there are no distinctions between fact and fiction, sanity and insanity, and worst of all between good and evil. There is no ordinary recognizable reality, and man, bereft of any standard to measure either his world or himself, finds that survival is the most he can hope for in coping with his waste land. Stanley Elkin's second novel, *A Bad Man*, takes away the last toehold on reality—the distinction between good and evil—and leaves us in total doubt that anything ordinary exists.[1] The hero of the book voices what has become the common cry of the sixties: "Everything goes on, he thought. *Why do you let everything go on?* he prayed." Where once we saw the world as *possibility*, and found it a cause for joy as many of the writers of the fifties did, now *possibility* is evidence that the world is anything, and we find that a cause for terror. Life can still be affirmed, but laughter seems even more necessary as the ambiguities and paradoxes multiply. The man who would affirm life must pull affirmation from the very causes and roots of paradox; he must, like Elkin's hero, be "made bold by his very fright, comforted by the magnitude of his terror and the slimness of his chances."

The story of *A Bad Man* is again the story of a confrontation between the individual and the institution. Here the idea of the waste land is symbolized by a jail, although the jail is as mad as any asylum conceived by Kesey. But even *its* madness is outdone by the individual in this case, for Elkin's hero—Feldman, the felled man, the heart's clown—is mad enough to be a bad man in a world that plays at goodness. As the novel opens Feldman is arrested for doing "favors." Later in the novel we learn that these favors were issued from the basement of his department store where Feldman gave out free service to his customers, supplying them with illegal abortion-

---

1. Page numbers for citations from *A Bad Man* will be included parenthetically in the text. Stanley Elkin has not yet been widely recognized, but I am confident he will be, for he stands out as one of the superior talents among recent writers.

ists, narcotics, and black market babies, with guns for would-be assassins, full military equipment for aroused right-wingers, and any other article he could offer to serve the morality of the mercantile world—"I consume, therefore I am." Feldman is taken off to jail, and the degrading treatment he receives at the hands of the deputy who transports him foreshadows the efforts that will be made in jail to reduce human dignity to the soft and the pliable.

In jail Feldman meets Warden Fisher, "Fisher of Bad Men." Feldman discovers that rapists, thieves, murderers, and criminals of almost all varieties are normal men, but he, for some inexplicable reason, which becomes his problem and our question, is considered a bad man. His stay in jail is a series of strange events that make him an unwilling and uncommitted combatant against the mysterious rule of Warden Fisher. He is thrown into Solitary, taken out to go to the Warden's party where he has intercourse with the Warden's wife, and ends the night by sleeping in a disconnected electric chair. He confronts the necessity of living among men who see him—in his specially made prison uniform, a clown's parody of his own suit—as a man to be purged. He gains insight into the meaning of goodness and badness and the madness of the world. He confronts his own wild past to examine his relationship to his mad Jewish father and his lumpy unloved wife, along with his child, his home, and his unbelievable business. In the end, as he reaches toward some control over his own carnivorous, expanding self, he is put on trial and convicted without reason or sense, but not without cause, and is executed by a pack of prisoners under the command of Warden Fisher, Fisher of Bad Men.

The jail has many of the characteristics we have already connected with the metaphor of the waste land: as one would expect of a jail, it works toward the ends of efficiency, acquiescence, and order; its iron bars teach men impotence, hopelessness, and a certain boredom relieved only by neurotic and vicious purges of the so-called bad men; it is a place of "maximum insecurity," where guilt and fear are again weapons in the hands of the institution to sterilize man of his individual impulses and his humanity; it is a "guilt factory"—it imposes a terrible set of complex, arbitrary, and inverted rules which, in truth, destroy any sense of reason or logic, but it imposes those rules in the name of "forms," "virtue," and "civilization." It teaches the prisoner hypocrisy and then imprisons him in every sense of the word, isolating him in the name of communal rehabilitation, and locking him inside a sense of shame for his hypocrisies. On an allegorical level, the jail is an appropriate image of everything that locks Feldman inside himself, and his fate echoes the words from "What the Thunder Said": "Dyadhvam: I have heard the key / Turn in the door once and turn once only."

Warden Fisher, like the Big Nurse in *One Flew over the Cuckoo's Nest,* is the authoritarian figure in whom all the destructive characteristics of the waste land institution are summed up. His concept of the "good" is the most terrifying thing about this waste land. "Virtue is system, honor is order. God is design, grace is covenant, a contract and codicils, what's down there in writing" (p. 70). The Warden's idea of virtue converts it not just to a system but to a system of ugly and brutal vengeance. He teaches his men "that virtue is as active a principle as evil, that cruelty is written off in a good cause, that there is no violence like an angel's violence" (p. 192). The Warden uses the name of goodness to teach his men

to spy on each other, to betray each other, and to actively
persecute each other. They become enervated victims
and victimizers in a system where anything goes, just as
long as it is covered with what the Warden frankly calls
"believable insincerity." Like any proper righteous lover
of the good, Warden Fisher prays to the god of his goodness, and his prayer forces us to recognize the potential
ugliness of the good.

> Lord God of hooked scourge and knotted whip, of
> sidearms and sidecar, of bloodhound and two-way
> radio, vigilant God of good neighborhoods and locked
> Heaven—lend us Thy anger. Teach us, O God, revul-
> sion. Remind our nostrils of stench and our ears of
> discord and our eyes of filth. Grant these men a holy
> arrogance and instill in them the courage to expose
> all bad men. [p. 192]

The prayer goes on through a sustained frenzy of violent apostrophes. Warden Fisher's idea of the good is
meant, obviously, to expose our own concept of the
good. Similarly, the effect of the good, as he imposes it
on his prisoners, is the effect we all suffer in our own
waste land prisons. It is the total loss of human dignity;
it is "to ignore inspiration, always to have second
thoughts. It is to live with the passions down, to move
through the world like someone sick whom the first cigar,
binge, fuck could kill. Finally—oh God, this was aston-
ishing, terrifying—it was to be *good*" (p. 32). In attempting to "renovate" his prisoners in accord with what is
"good," the Warden teaches them his view of the world.

> "Civilization is forms," he said. "It's also doing what
> you're told. It's knowing when enough is enough." [p.
> 183]

> Nothing is strange. Consecutive, the world is consecutive. It's rational. Life is ordinary. [p. 104]

But the real world of the prison is not "ordinary." It is more as Feldman describes it, "like coming to life in a Cubist sketch." It is overloaded with rituals and rules that lead the system to efficiency, and lead the men to impotent division among themselves. Its irrationality goes by the name of reason, and in some curious paradoxical way it is more like a "place of vicious, plodding sequiturs" that no one understands, than like the surreal world of its surface. What we come to understand beneath and because of all this overwhelming evidence is that the prison and Warden Fisher and the good are enemies of life and vitality.

The paradox of good and evil is intensified when we consider Feldman; he is the hero who opposes the institution and who is ultimately a life-affirming force, but he is by no means an angel. Feldman's ego is like the Diaspora that haunts him—it has dispersed and will go on dispersing until it has invaded all corners of the earth. Fedman is afflicted, we are told, with a four-inch shadow over his heart, a homunculus, a fetus, probably meant to be a twin but "some early Feldmanic aggrandizement" froze it and absorbed its life.[2] A blow on the chest and the homunculus will penetrate his heart instantly killing him. It is, we assume, such a blow that actually ends Feldman's life. The homunculus symbolizes the "locked heart" Feldman's father recognizes in him, and the carnivorous ego that absorbs but never gives. The homunculus itself tells Feldman, in a fantastical conversation while Feldman is in Solitary, that

2. Perhaps Elkin is sardonically playing with D. H. Lawrence's challenge in *Studies in Classic American Literature* for America to produce "the homunculus of the new era."

his heart is a "desert place"; "it won't support life." At the opposite pole from the Warden, Feldman the bad man is not guilty of self-righteous selflessness; Feldman is selfish. Frankly and openly he never thinks of anyone but himself, and he tells us so as he expresses disinterest in the other prisoners. When he reflects upon the gloom he has added to the world, he assures himself that he has picked on victims only, people who enjoy being victims, not people like himself. He betrays his friends, agonizes his wife, twists his child, and abuses them all in a series of such outlandishly funny actions that we cannot pick the pain from the laughter. The events are too numerous to list, but one reasonably short incident quoted in full may serve to illustrate; it is one of the many extraordinary games which Feldman bullies his wife, Lilly, and his child, Billy, into playing. This time at supper, they play "To Tell the Truth."

It's a game on television, where three people, all claiming to be the same person, answer questions about their lives for a panel, who then try to guess the right person. Feldman made Billy be the panel, and he and Lilly were the contestants. "My name is Lilly Feldman," he told the kid. "I married my husband, Leo Feldman, and came to live with him in this city, where he owns a department store." Then Billy had to ask questions. "Do you have a son?" he asked. "Yes," Feldman said, "his name is Billy." "Do *you* have a son?" he asked his mother. "Say 'Lilly Feldman number two,'" Feldman said. "She's Lilly Feldman number two, and I'm Lilly Feldman number one. You must say Lilly Feldman number one or number two." "Lilly Feldman number two," the kid said, "do you have a son?" "Yes," she said. "What's his name?" Feldman glowered at her, and she knew he meant for her to lie. So Lilly said, "His name is Charles." Billy asked more questions, and each time Feldman told the truth and made Lilly lie.

Finally Feldman said the time was up. "Which is it? Lilly Feldman number one or number two?" Billy was confused and shook his head. "Come on," Feldman said, "which is it? You heard the answers. Which is the real Lilly Feldman, that lousy imposter or me?" The kid finally pointed to his father, and Feldman said, "Will the real Lilly Feldman please stand up?" and both of them feinted for a couple of minutes until the kid was crying, and then Lilly stood up and went to him. [p. 318]

Feldman's indifference to others not only results in Billy's inability to pick the real Lilly from the fictional, but contributes to the book's overall vision of a world in which "anything happens." Feldman himself has no real sense of the ordinary or the everyday. He was brought up by an old Jewish merchant who made his money selling "stuff." Feldman recognized when he was still very young that his father was mad, and that he really made his money by an outlandish approach to sales—he sold children one crayon at a time with a lengthy metaphysical dissertation on each color, and he bullied adults into buying envelopes, string, and anything he got hold of, because his fantastic flights of language had gotten hold of them. Living with madness, Feldman grows up convinced the world makes no sense. He learns only mercantile values from his father whose entire vocabulary is made up of metaphors of business and selling. The meaning of life is "get what there is and turn it over quick." If everything exists in this world, it is because

"everything is vendible." The result is that Feldman becomes the perfect *amoral* man—not a bad man, and not
a good one either, but one who sees all things as equal
under the law of supply and demand, sell and get sold,
and always try to move "the unsalable thing." Feldman
even outstrips his father, for his father was mystified by
how to get rid of the "unsalable thing," which turns out
to be himself. But Feldman solves the mystery—he sells
his father's dead body for fifteen dollars. Feldman is the
perfect black humorist.

In the mad countinghouse of his world Feldman himself becomes a supersalesman who gloats over luxury,
and dips in and out of the piles of merchandise in his
own department store like his father diving into the stuff
of his pushcart, recalling cartoon character Scrooge Mc-
Duck swimming and surfacing like a porpoise in the pile
of money his vault holds. Feldman finds that "indulgence keeps a guy in condition. Afford, afford and enjoy.
Meaning of life, money in the bank." His activities in
his department store easily match his madness at home,
culminating in those famous bargain basement services
where he becomes a "moral fence." Amidst his tactile
splendor Feldman hates no man and loves no man; he
is totally uncommitted and his compassion extends no
further than his name on the letterhead of Charities.
He is an artist of the marketplace and the "master of all
he purveys." He is the artist Philip Roth evokes in the
article mentioned earlier—the artist who is in a constant
contest with *facts* to see who can get up the most convincing fiction. "It hadn't ever been profit that had
driven him, but the idea of the sale itself, his way of
bearing down on the world" (p. 266). As an artist, selling
is his way of dealing with the world. He becomes gradually more erratic as the book progresses because each

wild scheme and manipulation is accepted as normal and even occasionally topped by a world where madness seems the rule.

> For all that there were telephone poles about him, newspapers, machines, cars, neon in the windows of the taverns, he seemed to live in a world that might have been charted on an old map, the spiky spines of serpents rising like waves from wine-dark seas, personified zephyrs mump-cheeked and fierce—a distant Praetorianed land, unamiable and harsh. There might have been monkeys in the trees, burning bushes in the summers. He lived in constant fear of miracles that could go against him. [pp. 41–42]

The world that Feldman lives in is really the world of the entire novel, filled with details of the expected that somehow serve the fabulous. It is the vision we will see time and again in the novel of the sixties—an inverted mad world, "unamiable and harsh," where facts slip into and out of fiction as easily as Feldman slips in and out of his games, and where the sudden realization that anything is possible (because nothing is sure) becomes a fear of mysterious miracles that are probably out to get you. "Why balk at that?" Dr. Freedman asks Feldman who won't believe the awful miracle of his homunculus, "Everything's strange." But Feldman already knows that; it is really us Freedman is addressing.

The picture of Elkin's waste land should now be fairly clear. What remains to be explained is the quality of the opposition between Warden Fisher and Feldman, and the final relevance of Feldman's death. Warden Fisher, the Fisher of Bad Men, whose face is described as "lacking the vitality to grow hair," is wounded in terms of his vitality as one would expect the Fisher King to be wounded. But the Fisher King traditionally should be led back from the shadow of death and into life. Warden Fisher makes no such move and is more of an anti–Fisher King than anything else. If we could, however, imagine the Fisher King as incurable because he fails to recognize his disease and therefore rules his land by locking it in its wasted condition, and if we could imagine the Grail Knight sacrificed to such a Fisher King, we would have the image of the modern institution as waste land: full-blown irrationality that fails to see its sickness, even as it grows sicker, and that will not be cured no matter how hard we quest, no matter how much we sacrifice. Feldman is sacrificed, and though he himself affirms the mysteries of life and we do have some sense that life can win out over death, Warden Fisher does not allow a rebirth, nor is there any hope that he or his prison waste land will be cured or redeemed. Sacrifice becomes a gesture and a symbol that the sacrificer himself has been initiated into the mysteries of life-affirming potency— but he can have no effect on a waste land where resistance comes from the Fisher King himself. It is this kind of small symbolic affirmation that we see most often in the novels of the sixties, not the more complete success that McMurphy achieved in *One Flew over the Cuckoo's Nest.*

But what kind of Grail Knight is Feldman? A Parsifal he's not. Like McMurphy, Feldman is a doer, a pusher, a confronter; he is not the introspective hero of the past. Neither is he a *willing* sacrificer, and he has his own salesman's idea of a quest: "Riddled with need I was, hunting a piece of the action like a grapple of grail" (p. 327). Nonetheless, in his final moments Feldman transcends the bad man in himself and learns a new response to the texture of life. Understanding Feldman's progress from the apparent man of indifference to a man who can feel (if not give, sympathize, and control) can help us understand the relevance of his death; it can also demonstrate the novel's final vision of the possibility that man may cope with the waste land.

As in the beginning of Franz Kafka's *The Trial, A Bad Man* opens with the hero's arrest. The arrest has the same effect on Feldman as it has on Joseph K.—it halts the direction of his life and puts him onto a whole new set of perceptions about the world. For Feldman it is the arrest of his ego's expansion and the doom of the exclusively selfish character we have seen him to be. That does not mean his demanding self is laid to rest; indeed, the final moments leave that possibility ambiguous and perhaps imply the self will never stop its clamoring. But the book achieves one further paradox: through the attempts made by Warden Fisher—who sometimes does give the proper advice—and his jail to force Feldman into submission and thereby make him good, Feldman is driven into discovery and transcends the ambiguities of good and bad.

Feldman's first step out of indifference is his most telling step; he learns the value of life over death. "What he missed, he supposed, was the comfort of his old indifference when nothing counted and madness was all there was. Now there was a difference. It was because he counted; his *life* counted. It always had. How could it be? It didn't make sense" (p. 71). The point is well made. Nothing in this waste land makes sense—but life counts. Feldman begins to worry about the other convicts and listens to their stories. He learns what trouble means, and in learning has his first insight into the meaning of selfishness. "Feldman—thinking trouble was something outside, like a sudden freeze or extended drought; or something mechanical, like fouled ropes or defective brakes; or something inside and mechanical like a broken tooth or cholesterol deposits—met the bad man Herbert Mix" (p. 93). Herbert Mix is the stereotype of the man who wants his share, who irrationally demands he get something because he has nothing, has earned nothing, but deserves something because *you* earned something— not the oppressed and deprived man, just an inert but selfish man. Herbert Mix's selfishness directly endangers Feldman in prison business. So Feldman learns that selfishness equals trouble and that trouble is omnipresent —it is the same mystery of unknown forces that haunts the paranoia of the sixties. "He awoke. He sat up. *In trouble. As in atmosphere. Or in China.* It was an ambience, a dimension. Sure, he thought, the turd dimension. Something in nature. Something inside and mechanical. Something inside and not mechanical at all. Doom, he thought, the house struck by lightning, the wooden leg in flames, the poisoned heart" (p. 98). It is here Feldman realizes that seeing the world as everything is more a matter of terror than of hope or indifference. He begins to try goodness—motivated, at least in part, by a desire to regain control—but is a wretched failure and ends only by recognizing the immensity of the Warden's power. Warden Fisher's institutional waste land provides a target but cannot be defeated, for the Fisher King has become keeper of the waste and he has all the sick power, even as the Warden tells Feldman:

> We have *investigators,* the crime labs. We have the law and the rules, don't you see? We keep the records and have the radios and the alarm systems and the TV over the teller's cage. We have the cells and the jails and the institutions. We have the speed zones and the

traffic signals and the alternate-side-of-the-street parking regulations. We have the magnified maps of the
city, the pins in the colored neighborhoods. We have
the beats and patrols. We have the system. Virtue is
system. [p. 70]

Feldman's real confrontation with his own ego's selfishness, with "the punishment of himself," occurs after his
attempt at goodness, while he is in solitary. He begins
with a wild orgy of masturbation and calls it the most
satisfying sex life he has had; Solitary itself he terms "a
god damn love nest." It is an apt symbol for Feldman's
whole life to that point—an orgy of self-love. He never
does put an end to this appetite of the self, but he does
begin to discover a love turned outward toward the
world. When the masturbating stops Feldman has the
terrifying recognition that his life has had and still does
have an "inferior quality." Once out of Solitary, Feldman again tries to capture the "virtue of the routinized
life," but it ends abruptly when he has intercourse with
the Warden's wife in the Warden's bedroom at the
Warden's party. Feldman does not know who the woman
is at the time of the act, but he proves himself a truly
bad man in the Warden's eyes—not because of adultery,
but because he has brought vitality and potency into the
stronghold of death's defender. For this Feldman is cast
into Hell—the Warden's basement, home of the electric
chair. In that hell Feldman comes to grips with death
itself. He realizes he has been uncommitted and "mealy-
hearted," and that it is not the Warden who plots his
death but he himself—"It was true; he wanted his death.
He wanted his death because it was coming to him and
he wanted everything that was coming to him" (pp.
179–80). Feldman straps himself to the electric chair and

waits to get his charge, but it does not come. So he lives, and yet: "what he had felt about death was perhaps all he could ever feel. If that was so, then now, in a way, he didn't have to die. Ever" (p. 181). Feldman has both learned the value of life and lost the fear of death. But when he ascends from the basement, he finds his ordeal, the ordeal of the Grail Knight, is not over; in fact, his trial has just begun.

The actual trial is no trial at all. There is no pretense of justice—Feldman is doomed. He has always been doomed, because to be a bad man means to want to live, to be a vital active force. It has nothing to do with good or bad; in fact, in Feldman's world it is impossible to be life-affirming and not be the amoral man he has been, for we have seen what goodness means. So the trial makes no pretense at justice—it is a ritual, "a ceremony of denouncement, a process of judgment." But as much as Feldman is unwilling to die, he has armed himself for this last ordeal in the Chapel Perilous. When he first entered the jail he told us that "to lose freedom meant to become visible." Just before the trial Feldman reiterates the image of the invisible man, recognizing at least that his invisibility is not a good thing—even putting aside the doubtful freedom, it has made his life a constant flight from contact. Although he fails to understand whose fault it is that he is invisible, Feldman is led to express an almost religious reverence for life itself.

All life, all history, what he has been, what he was now, the stars and everything in books, all the wars that had ever happened, the reason behind things he never questioned, the facts about electricity and the skeletons of beasts and the mystery of God, were contained for him in the few drops of soapy water he felt this moment

splash on the back of his hand as he dipped his scrub
brush into the pail beside him and scrubbed and
prayed to the floor of his cell. [p. 303]

This new form of Feldman's love of life becomes his de-
fense—it is all he has against the warden's men and their
fatal accusations.

There remains only the last passion of this modern version of the Grail Knight. In it, Feldman defends himself
and tries to make contact with others—he tries to make
himself visible. He sings to his judges a Whitmanesque
song of all things, of the entire texture of life—a song
which, considering Feldman, may very well be a song
of himself, but a song that shows he has loved, and felt,
and had an emotional life. It is an amazing catalog of
the familiar texture of human activities (unfortunately,
far too long to quote), which shows Feldman's real love
of all things. He has had compassion; he has not been
unstirred. When finished, "his face had undergone a
remarkable change—his passion visible now, open wide
as the groan on a tragic mask" (p. 322). But Feldman
is not understood, and the Warden looses his men
upon him to preserve "goodness" through the sacrifice
of life.

Perhaps Feldman had locked himself away too long
(trying to "bear down on the world") to become visible
now. We are, however, provided with an interesting
analogy that helps us understand one more difference between the novel of the fifties and that of the sixties. Ralph
Ellison's brilliant *Invisible Man* ends with the narrator
underground, discovering that he has been invisible because he has allowed himself to be invisible—a perception
similar to Feldman's. But despite the chaos of a riot going
on above him, and despite a world that has rejected him

entirely, Ellison's narrator makes an existential leap that
carries him to responsibility, and then right up out of his
hole. The world, we take it, will now cooperate in one
way or another. Feldman's world—the world of the sixties
—is no longer so manageable. Feldman is done in by the
intractable life-opposing mystery, symbolized by the institution, just when he too comes out of his hole. It is as
if Feldman, imitating Ellison's narrator, were torn to
bits the moment he made his leap. The difference is in
man's sense of control. Feldman can control himself, but
only after a long struggle and with no hope of gaining
any wider control. For Ellison's narrator, control of himself guarantees control of the world. We have lost ground;
the world is irrevocably set against us. The difference is
not a simple difference of vision between Elkin and Ellison, but a paradigm of one difference between a vision
characteristic of the fifties and a vision characteristic of
the sixties.

Much about the ending of Elkin's book is ambiguous.
In the last moments, Feldman feels assured he is innocent,
and in his death he "filled the world." The narrator never
makes us certain that Feldman is innocent, or certain that
in filling the world Feldman is filling it with his new
compassion instead of performing one last magnificent
"Feldmanic aggrandizement." It is possible that Feldman
—even as an exile—has really achieved unity with the
world; as Joseph Campbell puts it:

> The essence of oneself and the essence of the world:
> these two are one. Hence separateness, withdrawal, is
> no longer necessary. Wherever the hero may wander,
> whatever he may do, he is ever in the presence of his
> own essence—for he has the perfected eye to see. There
> is no separateness. Thus, just as the way of social par-

ticipation may lead in the end to a realization of the All in the individual, so that of the exile brings the hero to the Self in all.[3]

We are not even sure, however, that Feldman is dead—not completely sure, anyway. Ultimately all such questions are transcended by Feldman's initiation, as Grail Knight, into the mysteries of life-affirming potency. But before that initiation occurs, Feldman abandons, rather than transcends, the traditional American hero's search for pure freedom, proving its irrelevance—or downright danger—to our times. When he does hunt freedom, it is not in the west of America; he hunts it through the absolute expansion of the self, so that he allows none of society's repressions and inversions to impinge on him, nor compassion, commitment, or responsibility to limit him. Such selfish freedom literally puts Feldman in jail and leads him to discover that the perfectly expanded self, the pure search for freedom, paradoxically results in an imprisoned self, even when it is successful. Thus, the really vital quest in the novel does not begin until he is in prison—until he is confronted with the waste land—and then the object of the quest is no longer freedom. It is as if entering the jail, entering the waste land, signals the end of the American Dream. The single important quest is for a way to cope with the waste land, for a way to affirm the fertility of life itself against overwhelmingly negative forces, and that quest involves setting aside the paradoxes of good and evil along with the fruitless desire for pure freedom. Feldman's way of coping involves three methods most common to the novel of the sixties: the black humorist's laughter, a necessarily

3. *The Hero with a Thousand Faces* (New York: World Publishing Co., Meridian Books, 1949), p. 386.

violent demonstration of his humanity, and affirmation through the individual's purely symbolic gesture.

Feldman's sacrifice and his magnificent refusal to recognize anything but life, even to the point that he speaks continuously of life as death descends upon him, are what I mean by affirmation through purely symbolic gesture. The gesture does not alter the waste land, but it proves Feldman to himself, and it gives us a momentary sense of control through stability achieved in a symbolic transcending of tensions. We have glimpsed madness and death, and through Feldman we have chosen life.

Feldman is able to maintain his hold on life-affirmation only by resisting the waste land's definition of the good and that can only be accomplished by violent means: by madness, by self-love, and by inflicting pain as if it were a pinch in the middle of a nightmare, proving you can still be awake. His skirmishes with his wife and his betrayal of Dedman, uncompassionate as those responses are, still do force Lilly and Dedman to be "on their feet and slugging," as George provokes Martha to be in *Who's Afraid of Virginia Woolf?* Feldman forces a little life into Lilly's otherwise extraordinarily boring existence and makes Dedman more than a Dedman for at least a little while. Elkin makes no apology for his hero's badness, for the real measure of the forces against life is the extremity a hero is forced to in affirming life —exorcism becomes the only possible act of love, and madness is the only true preserver of sanity.

Laughter in *A Bad Man* is a theme achieved through technique. Unlike Ken Kesey, Elkin does not theorize about laughter, but it is everywhere in his book. It is used, as the bulk of the writers in the sixties use it—in black humor, mixing it with pain, stirring our consciences without moralizing, and gaining some control over the despair that threatens to hand the plaguey mess over to everyone's Warden Fisher. In one parenthetical comment, Feldman mentions laughter: "It is in the long sad tradition of my people to pluck laughter from despair." Even as Feldman says it, Elkin means it, demonstrates it, and mocks it; this is, in small, an example of how he uses laughter.

Because *A Bad Man* removes what I called at the beginning of this chapter the last toehold on reality—the formal distinctions between good and evil—it is a good example of the kind of fable that was written in the sixties. It is not really a creation of fantastical characters moving in a fantastical world for the sake of escape or to illustrate abstract moral principle. It is a demonstration of what is fabulous about the actual world we live in. Filled with moments that shock us with their seeming fidelity to the known (like the mock TV program quoted earlier), the book drives us back and forth from saying it is no world we know to saying it is exactly the world we know. *A Bad Man* removes all doubt that abstractions about Meaning could have any value. It is simply a world incredibly fabulous, filled with some force called Warden Fisher that overwhelms us, but against which we can still say with Feldman that life is worth affirming. Faced with so vast a confusion between fact and fiction, good and evil, life and death, and faced with a choice between Fisher's sterility and Feldman's madness, all that can be said is what Feldman's secretary tells him: "The world is getting to be a terrible place, and I don't know if it's your kind or their kind who makes it more awful, but if we must have terror, let it be gay and exciting, I say" (p. 295).

3: THE GRAIL KNIGHT GOES TO COLLEGE

Stanley Elkin's hero, Feldman, has no chance to redeem anyone but himself, nor does he make any effort to. The waste land of his world remains blighted although Feldman himself transcends its paradoxes and contradictions. The impossibility of redeeming a waste land that has become one vast institution is made even clearer in John Barth's *Giles Goat-Boy*, where the hero does actively seek to redeem the world, and where the waste land institution is a universal university. George GILES, Goat-boy and Grand-Tutorial Ideal, transcends questions and paradoxes, as Feldman did, to achieve some peace and to be symbolically reborn in the belly of WESCAC, the ultimate computer.

But George wants to redeem everybody; he is not satisfied with symbolic affirmation. For that reason there is a "Posttape" to his first-person narrative, tape-recorded gospel, and it contradicts what seems to be the achieved peace, affirmation, and success of the story proper. In the Posttape George is bitter, tired, and ready for his crucifixion. Despite what he had achieved earlier, he has failed as a world redeemer; his despondency leaves in doubt even the one possibility that the private individual by himself, like Feldman, can ever be redeemed. George's final gesture in the Posttape is a microcosm of Barth's overall attitude: it characterizes a redeemer while it parodies redeemers; it offers a symbolic resolution while it parodies the device of symbolic resolution; it completes an image of an unredeemed waste land while it parodies the final moments of Eliot's *Waste Land*.[1] Barth uses parody to express his version of black humor, taking everything for his target (even what he affirms), and asserting both the truth and the absurdity of these targets. Consequently, in place of the sacred sounds that signify the achievement of peace—the "Shantih, shantih, shantih," spoken by the Thunder at the end of Eliot's *Waste Land*—Barth has George, in his last gesture, anticipate his own crucifixion: at that time his parts will be "hung with mistletoe," and the shophar that will carry the sacred sounds will be held fast in his cleft. Then will George meet his end, as he tells us: "The oak will yield, the rock know my embrace. Three times will lightning flash at a quarter after seven, all the University bespeaking my love's thunder" (p. 708), and then the sacred sounds as the thunder speaks—"Teruah! Tekiah! Shebarim!" sounded from the shophar as George blows it through his ass.

George's quest has two phases and two endings (both of which, incidentally, are called into further doubt by a Postscript to the Posttape and a Footnote to the Postscript to the Posttape). Like Eliot's Tiresias, George narrates his own failure and is transformed from Grail Knight to wounded Fisher King. At 21, when the story

1. Richard Poirier has also made the suggestion that Barth is parodying the closing moments of *The Waste Land*. See "WESCAC and the Messiah," in *The World of Black Humor*, ed. Douglas M. Davis (New York: Dutton, 1967), p. 328.

proper ends, George seems to have completed his quest, but at 33⅓, in the Posttape, he reveals his failure to redeem the University, which has led him to bitter despair and to the loss of his own personal salvation. What happens to George to change him from Grail Knight to wounded Fisher King? The question is a crux in Barth's book. The change can best be understood by looking at the nature of George's quest and the nature of the waste land world he faces—the universe as university.

Early in his life George learns from his guardian, Max Spielman, two propositions about the world he lives in: (1) "Spielman's Law of Cyclology" in which "ontogeny recapitulates cosmogeny," or the history of the individual recapitulates the history of the University; and (2) "West Campus [George's World] as a whole is in mid-adolescence." George's quest is simply the search for maturity, which, according to Spielman's Law, means he is searching for his own personal maturity and that of his world. "What hope there was that such an adolescent would reach maturity (not to say Commencement) without destroying himself was precisely the hope of the University." [2] Initiation into personal maturity should, George believes, equip him for the second phase of his quest— the redemption of the world, to be accomplished when the world is brought to its maturity. Barth places a great deal of emphasis on the world's need for maturity, and his idea of what constitutes initiation into maturity is somewhat complex. To be mature does not mean a simple accommodation to the reality principle. It is an initiation into the mysteries of the Grail, an affirmation of life based on the acceptance of death as a part of life; it is to be able to love, be loved, and feel a sense of unity

2. *Giles Goat-Boy*, p. 255. Page numbers for all further citations will be included parenthetically in the text.

with the "seamless" university, to achieve the peace that goes with harmony; and it is to wrest ultimate control over one's own destiny away from whatever force has it in hand. George achieves all these things at the moment of his initiation, but having earned his own maturity, he expects to teach the answers to everyone. It seems a reasonable expectation since "teaching" is the major mode of adult activity in a world that is all university. George guesses that bringing the world to maturity and redeeming it will involve saving it from self-destruction. To save the world he need only conquer WESCAC with its capacity to "EAT" all mankind. (The ultimate weapon, Electroencephalic Amplification and Transmission—EAT—destroys the human mind en masse.) WESCAC, however, has gained the power to program itself and to decide by itself when to use its ultimate weapon; thus it has the power of life and death over man.

By pinpointing WESCAC as the obstacle to maturity and redemption, George seems to have found the answer to the question raised so often in the novel of the sixties —what has seized control over man's life? Through a great part of the book he is led to believe that WESCAC is the single enemy, but the computer, as he discovers, is not ultimately the true location of control in the University. George's quest for maturity and his progress in that quest are measured by his comprehension of the forces that control his life. That progress also provides the basic structure for Barth's narrative movement, and he works it out semiseriously on at least two levels beyond the overt allegory and the story line—the mythological level and the psychological level. Barth parodies and responds to two of Eliot's major indictments against the waste land —the failure to believe in a mythology and the psychological failure to unify our sensibilities.

George's life as a hero is a devised and constructed mythology based to some extent on Lord Raglan's description of a hero and Joseph Campbell's history of a hero's archetypal actions. Barth's use of Raglan's categories is clear enough to need no comment, but a look at how he has played with Joseph Campbell's "monomyth"—played with it deliberately and by his own admission[3]—can tell us something about George's quest for maturity and his ultimate transformation from successful Grail Knight to wounded Fisher King. The hero, as Campbell describes him and Barth transcribes him, goes through a three-part ritual that functions as a passage from adolescence to maturity—the three parts are: "departure," "initiation," and "return." Barth alters this pattern to allow for the static world of the institution. So "departure" means a movement not from one world to another but from one part of campus to another, and "return" means only George's attempt to teach what he has experienced. There is no possibility of leaving the University; instead, George remains trapped in the waste land and is transformed to an ailing Fisher King. The static nature of George's world prevents any kind of real voyage; and the necessary rebirth of the hero, which takes place according to Campbell in a womb symbolized by the belly of a whale, occurs according to Barth in the belly of a computer. The whale's belly provides a perfect moving womb for a hero who journeys, but the hero trapped in a static institution must make do with the unmoving WESCAC.

3. Barth himself has informed us of his fascination with Campbell's tradition of the wandering hero. He said in an interview, "The only way I could use it would be to make it comic, and there will be some of that in *Giles Goat-Boy*." See "John Barth: An Interview," *Wisconsin Studies in Contemporary Literature* 6 (Winter–Spring 1965): 3–14.

Campbell's "departure" and "initiation," however, do
provide a rough structural basis for the steps of George's
progress, and a further field for Barth's brand of parody.
"The call to adventure" initiates the hero's awareness of
"an unsuspected world," drawing him "into a relationship with forces that are not rightly understood." [4] Any
kind of herald will do to stir the hero, and Barth multi-
plies the calls to George. He is summoned from Goat
Barn to Campus Mall: by one herald named G. Herrold,
the kindly Negro who saved George when he was an
infant; by a series of Oedipal dreams; by some stimula-
tions from Lady Creamhair—his first lady human; and
by a long climactic blast on the Campus EAT-whistle.
The second step, Campbell tells us, provides the hero
with amulets and supernatural aid from some little old
crone—Max Spielman is the little old crone who ties the
amulet of Freddie's testicles around George's waist. Then
the hero is ready to cross the "First Threshold." George
gets across "George's Gorge" on the shoulders of the
giant savage Croaker, who has responded to Anastasia's
thrust-up smock. George does some more threshold cross-
ing when he gets through the Campus Turnstile naked.
Campbell's next step calls for rebirth in the belly of the
whale, but Barth saves that for the climax of George's
initiation.

"Initiation" begins for Campbell's hero with "The
Road of Trials." George, continuing his comic pursuit of
herohood, engages in seven tasks, each done twice and
each round resulting in disaster, chaos, and a lynching.
After each disastrous completion of the seven tasks, George
makes a hopeful trip to the Belly of WESCAC, but only
on the third trip does he complete his initiation, combining two of Campbell's steps—"The Meeting with the

4. Campbell, *The Hero with a Thousand Faces*, p. 386.

Goddess" and "Atonement with the Father." Anastasia turns out to be the Goddess, and WESCAC, of all things, turns out to be the Father. The meeting with the goddess is the final trial of the hero because it tests his ability to win the "boon of love," to understand that divinity, life, and love are identical, and that all must be approached through the goddess, woman, who is the vessel of love—the grail bearer. United with the goddess Anastasia near the end of the story proper, George makes what seems to be a discovery that fulfills Campbell's pattern instead of parodying it; George learns he is loved: " 'Wonderful!' I cried. For though the place was lightless, and my head pursed, in Anastasia I discovered the University whole and clear" (p. 672). When WESCAC asks its usual question—"ARE YOU MALE OR FEMALE"—George, united with Anastasia as one, need not answer, because in maturity he has become both male and female. He is Tiresias before his failure in the Hyacinth Garden—the complete and whole human, the fulfilled Grail Knight, who in discovering a sense of oneness with all things has discovered the Grail, been initiated into the mysteries of life-affirmation, and achieved the "peace which passeth understanding." "The mystical marriage with the queen goddess of the world," as Campbell says, "represents the hero's mastery of life." [5] George need not answer WESCAC because he has conquered it, short-circuited it. Through this experience of unity he is "atoned with the father" in the sense that WESCAC's Belly has provided the womb for George's second birth. The total experience, including wresting power from his father, WESCAC, in order to be ruler of his own destiny, signifies George's passage into maturity. From there he ends the story by chasing out Bray, who on the mythological

5. Ibid., p. 120.

level is simply the adversary, on ogre, a troll, who must be banished to complete George's maturity and mastery. (On the psychological level, as we shall see, Bray has a somewhat more complicated significance.) George has completed the first phase of his quest and the story ends on a triumphant note as he prepares for the work of his adult life—redemption of the Campus.

But the myth is not completed. Campbell tells us: "The hero of yesterday becomes the tyrant of tomorrow, unless he crucifies himself today. From the point of view of the present there is such a recklessness in this deliverance of the future that it appears to be nihilistic." [6] This explains George's attitude in the Posttape. He has finally understood the truth of Spielman's Law of Cyclology. The mythological cycle involving a hero's passage to maturity may have successfully completed itself, but George makes the personal discovery that he is only a cog in that cycle. In a sense he does not have mastery over his own life—he is subject to the mystery of cycles. He has not only failed to redeem the Campus, which is in a decidedly descending phase of the eternal cycle, but he has been merely an "emblematic," not a "practical," hero. (The distinctions are made by Max and Dr. Sear—practical heroes are "those who in fact or fiction rendered some extraordinary service to studentdom"; emblematic heroes are "those whose careers were merely epical representations of the ordinary life-cycle, or the daily psychic round, or whatever—a dramatical metaphor, if we would" [pp. 263–64].) By giving us the story of a redeemer from the first-person point of view, Barth is able to continue his parody of mythologies, of *The Waste Land,* of heroic Gospels, and of that favorite device in the novel of the sixties—symbolic resolution.

6. Ibid., p. 353.

George is unhappy about being a part of a cycle, being a ritual "Hanged God," being a symbol, an "emblematic hero"; he wants to redeem the waste land in fact. Symbolic gestures may indicate individual affirmation of life, but they go nowhere in solving the problems of the University. So George loses the peace he has achieved, and his bitterness becomes a wound. In the Posttape, he may be preparing for his crucifixion and actually completing the mythological cycle—a cycle which explains even his nihilism—but on the personal level his attitude also reveals he has become the ailing Fisher King, complaining much as Eliot's Tiresias complains that life worsens and religion fails. "If New Tammany's new Auditorium has no flogging-room beneath it, neither has it a soaring campanile above" (p. 707). The ambiguities of Barth's double ending are multiplied when we realize that George, even in the Posttape, continues to be a success mythologically, affirming the eternally mysterious cycle that has included Christ and Buddha, while he is nonetheless a failure on the personal and psychological level. Losing even the peace and sense of unity he achieved in the Belly of WESCAC, George is beset by a bitchy Anastasia, certainly no longer a goddess of love, and seems to have failed both himself and the University in his quest for maturity. Once again man loses the mastery of his own life to some mysterious force—a force that is not so simple as a computer.

In the meantime, the mythology of "The Revised New Syllabus" is created despite George's contempt for it. If George, and the reader, could believe in this or any other mythology, another rehearsal of the cycle would be a comfort. However, even George admits the mythology of The Revised New Syllabus is an "invention." We are forced to recognize that Barth's creation of a mythology —a parody even in its serious moments—reveals our inability to accept Mythology. And further, the university waste land, fathering our ultra faith in rational consciousness, prevents the acceptance of mythology, which to be accepted must be the genuine creation of the unconscious. Barth's conscious mythology flaunts the failure of mythology in the modern world as it openly announces its complete contrivance. The university is the perfect image of the waste land in this case; it is responsible, at least symbolically, for our desire to find answers and for our overconsciousness. Thus, the university and George's world become a waste land because he and the reader see the existence of cycles not as a proof that there is a benevolent divine order, but rather as an indication that man has lost control over his own life to some mystery which is nothing more than the principle of repetition.

George is right about one thing: maturity, bringing with it an acceptance of the cycle of life and death and a feeling of unity with the world, can restore man's sense of mastery over his own life and redeem man from his waste land. On the psychological level, Barth's concern with the world's mid-adolescence becomes even clearer. George is both Grail Knight and Everyman; he is going through the psychological movement from adolescence to maturity and his goal is the same as the goal of mythology —to be one with the world and thereby achieve peace and self-mastery. The problems of maturity are the problems of how to heal the conflicts created by the long period of dependence in human infancy, how to deal with the repression of the pleasure principle, and how to look forward in life rather than back toward the "polymorphous sexual perversity" of childhood.[7] Maturity, in one sense,

7. For the psychological framework, I have relied upon Norman O. Brown, *Life against Death* (New York: Random House, Modern Library, 1959), and Sigmund Freud, *An Outline of Psychoanalysis*, trans. by James Strachey (New York: Norton, 1949).

means finding some way to play without regressing to childhood in order to do it. Barth's characters indulge in a variety of sexual activities which, despite the appearance of depraved sophistication, only prove their desire to be childlike, and offer no genuine "instinctual release" from repression. Even sexual freedom, parodied by Barth in the characters he calls "Beists," offers no release since adult sexuality is automatically an "organized genital activity" and no amount of indulgence will turn it back into the polymorphous activities of infancy. Maturity, then, does not lie in being "modern" about sex. Indeed, according to Norman O. Brown, maturity is close to impossible, for it involves the reunification of man's instinct for life (wrapped up in the concept of play) and his instinct for death (manifested in the simple desire for peace).

To simplify drastically, let us ask the question Brown continually asks, a question very pertinent to George, the Goat-Boy. "What had to happen to an animal in order to make him into a man-animal? . . . The essence of the man-animal is neurosis, and the essence of neurosis is mental conflict. The human neurosis must be traced to an instinctual ambivalence, a conflict between forces inherent in all organic life." [8] George, as a model of everyman, moves from an animallike unification of instincts, when he is a happy young goat, to the dizzying conflicts of human life, when he reaches Main Campus. To be mature he must achieve a reunification of instincts, but on a higher level than as a child. In a sense, he must seek to heal the familiar "dissociation of sensibilities," or to achieve that state of being which Wordsworth felt was "abundant recompense" for the loss of childhood joy. Belief in a mythology could help achieve this reunifica-

8. Brown, *Life against Death*, p. 82.

tion, or it could be achieved through the experience of union with some object other than the self—through love George becomes whole, for "Eros contains in itself the possibility of reunification with its opposite, and it strives toward that goal." [9] When George leaves the Belly, he is able to chase out Bray, who on the psychological level may very well stand for childhood play become loathful. Bray, whose speedy changes of identity are always related to George's personal world, could possibly be the principle of polymorphous sexual perversity. He has become twisted because he has no place in the adult world. Thus, George's maturity requires that he chase out this regressive principle.

One again, the experience in the Belly should mean that George has achieved maturity, but the Posttape demonstrates that his maturity is a tenuous thing. He must not only put aside his purse full of childish amulets, as he does before leaving the Belly for the last time, but he must maintain touch with that sense of unity gained so briefly with Anastasia. Only then will he really be mature. Otherwise, he has only ceased to be young. The pessimism of the Posttape indicates that maturity is not a state to be arrived at once and so achieved for all time. The point of the psychological level in *Giles Goat-Boy* is that man's condition makes maturity nearly impossible, and so George's quest is eternally doomed. Just as George could not be comforted by the knowledge that he was part of a cycle, he cannot hold on to that single "spot of time" when love supplied unity, maturity, and the peace which passeth understanding. What we see in the Posttape is not just a man who has failed to redeem others, and not just the inside story of a soon-to-be-hung savior (although it is both of these things too); what we see is a man whose

9. Ibid., p. 133.

maturity has soured and become only what is left after the principle of play, manifested in Eros, has gone out of life. In fact, when Max *Spielman* (play-man) goes up in smoke to end the story proper, George's ability to play also seems to have burned out. He is, indeed, transformed to the failed Fisher King. The real pessimism of this final glimpse at George lies in our knowledge that his wound is our wound unless we can accept the symbolic affirmation that comes in a moment's experience of unity, or be comforted in the knowledge that our life is a part of an eternal cycle—one that includes our death.

The mythological level and the psychological level come together in Barth's use of an Oedipal theme. For Barth the major significance of the Oedipal stage is that the child is in combat with the father for mastery of the world; by conquering the father he achieves his own identity, becomes father to himself and master of his fate. Again, George's quest for maturity demonstrates that both the individual and the world are somehow stuck in the Oedipal stage. Barth tells us this, still half in parody, as another way of expressing the overriding concern in the novel of the sixties—the individual's desire to snatch mastery of his life away from whatever has gained control of it. Besides George's struggle with the father-computer—an apt image of one of those powers we all blame for having taken over our lives—the book contains repeated blatant references to Oedipus and the Oedipus complex. George attacks Max as a surrogate father; George is summoned to his quest by Oedipal dreams and by his attempted rape of Lady Creamhair, who turns out to be his mother; George achieves his identity and the right to sign his own I.D. card when he unites with Anastasia, short-circuiting his father, WESCAC; and, lest we fail to notice all this, an entire production of *Oedipus Rex* is transferred to university terminology.

George's birth and his final moments also parody the life of Oedipus, from clubfoot to tragic fate. Nearly everyone he meets has Oedipal eye problems, and George himself is finally doomed to failure, not because he attempts to redeem himself and control his own fate, but because he is blind enough to attempt to redeem all men. In that quest, the one that leads to bitterness and loss of peace, George is guilty of hubris, for the message of love and the experience of unity are unteachable. Each man must be his own redeemer, must conquer the forces that rule him, and must move himself beyond the Oedipal stage to maturity. George's mistaken impulse to teach is integral with the image of the universe as university. He is not transformed to a wounded Fisher King after his youthful success as a Grail Knight just so Barth can complete the cycle—the waste land is unredeemable because redemption cannot be taught and man forever fools himself that the pursuit of learning is the sure way to maturity and salvation. The image of the university as waste land assists Barth in demonstrating what really has seized control over man's life: man's educated consciousness in conspiracy with his instinctual death wish has left him inert, unable to act, unable to accept mythology and its cycles, unable to achieve peace through the single moment's experience of unity, and unable to do even what George does—seek his own redemption instead of merely learning about it. This tendency to be inert or inanimate, the vitiated power to act that haunts Eliot's Tiresias, is, as we shall see in the coming chapters, a major theme in the novel of the sixties.

The terms of Barth's allegory are transparent enough; their importance lies in pointing out that the failure to believe in a mythology or to reunify our sensibilities—two of Eliot's major indictments in *The Waste Land*—has been the result of an overdeveloped consciousness. Peter Greene, Max, and Leonid argue for hours over abstractions, categories, and distinctions—but all the while they argue they languish needlessly in jail, taking no action at all. In this sense, Barth uses the university as an organic part of his vision, not just as an in-joke for a specialized audience. His terminology does pin down something otherwise elusive about the way we live; for example: to "Pass" or to "Fail" means to arrive at certain abstract states of grace or damnation, but as secular counterparts for religious concepts the words have no meaning because they are tied to no real value system. Passing represents that longing in us to "make it," to get a good grade in life-living so we can, for some reason unknown to us, have a better record than the other guy. Knowledge has replaced religion and mythology, and has produced a consciousness that is not content to simply *be*, but seeks to *pass*, indicating our continued wish for any state of grace that will assure us we have arrived at a purposeful ending to our efforts. Make it with all your might, baby, and though you won't go to heaven, you may Pass. Barth's parody of passing and failing demonstrates what proportions the American Dream has shrunk to—aspiration in a world with no values and no ends becomes an end in itself, a substitute for a meaningful life. (We saw this same frantic and useless idea of aspiration in Elkin's *A Bad Man,* and we will see it again in Joseph Heller's *Catch-22* and Thomas Pynchon's *V.*)

For Barth, the university is a reflection of the human condition, and while it may appear to be a force external to man—like WESCAC—it is really the creation of man's own inner ambiguities. Despite the University's seemingly unreconcilable contraries—symbolized by East Campus/West Campus, Eierkopf/Croaker, Rexford/Stoker, Spielman/Sear—George, the Grail Knight, temporarily puts to rest the conflicts of the University and of man's ambiguous nature. The individual can possibly be redeemed—although for George even that is temporary—but the University itself will remain a waste land. In order to be reborn in the Belly of WESCAC, George first goes through a series of revelations about the "student condition." In effect, he has to learn not to learn, and because he is a Goat-boy, because he has been raised to accept his goatishness as a beginning, George finds it easier than most of us do to launch out and learn through action. If George is really any kind of a hero, it is only his willingness to plunge on and continue to act that makes him so. His delayed maturity, as well as his ultimate bitterness, is caused by an erroneous desire to formulate his experience. It is for that reason he must do his seven tasks twice. The first time he operates under the principle that there must be clear distinctions between "passage" and "failure." The second time he devises a contrary principle—there are no distinctions. "Passage is failure." All things, then, are of equal value. When he applies these principles to other people's lives, urging them to live first by one and then by the other, the result is chaos and George gets two "failures" and two good sound lynchings. Finally, in an experience in "George's Gorge," when Stoker yells out to George not to try escaping, George escapes from his desire to seek answers and devise principles. He realizes that the University cannot examine him; he must examine himself. Then he is ready to complete his initiation by becoming one with Anastasia and the entire student body. In the story proper, he no longer gives advice. There are no answers to give. Each man must achieve his own maturity; as George puts it, his A and Bray's A would be of equal value on the Founder's Transcript.

As a student George learned the limitations of teaching and the uselessness of Answers, but as a teacher he, like so many teachers, forgets what it is like to be a student. In the Posttape he tries to teach even though he claims to recognize the futility, and he becomes embittered by his failure to redeem others. Yet, if he has failed to redeem studenthood, it is because the Student Condition forbids it. It is for this reason that parody is an important part of Barth's method and vision, for he parodies all of George's quest, parodies mythology, parodies psychology, and parodies even didacticism—thus leaving us with a story in which a life has been lived, but from which we dare learn nothing about how we should live ours. The lesson of the University is that life is livable, not learnable. George completes the cycle of the crucified redeemer, having guaranteed its continuance by conceiving a child with Anastasia at that very moment when he achieves maturity—in the Belly of WESCAC—and he completes the cycle of Grail Knight to Fisher King. So, we return to Founder's Hill where we began, with George clutching the shophar in his cleft, mocking the cycles that assure the continuance of life even as he fulfills them.

Barth's allegory is another way of expressing the modern confusion between fact and fiction. The terms of his allegory reveal that the fabulous world he creates is our world with our history, our politics, and our politicians. A great deal of the book speaks for itself because it is a fable. Like other fables of the sixties, Barth's book mixes the recognizable with the extreme—current world events with goat-boy saviors—so we are forced to admit that both or neither are possible, and that contemporary fact itself is fabulous, distinguishable from fiction only because the author has made his contrivance obvious. Barth himself has claimed that one "way to come to terms with the discrepancy between art and the Real Thing is to *affirm* the artificial element in art (you can't get rid of it anyhow), and make the artifice part of your point." [10] Barth's point is that life is fabulous, and with only a few contrivances of language, fact can be turned into "allegory." When George tells us of his attitude toward fact and fable he seems to be speaking for Barth—and he could be speaking for a great many novels in the sixties.

> For the most part I regarded natural laws with the same provisional neutrality with which one regards the ground-rules of a game or the exposition of a fable, and the reflection that one had no choice of games whatever (when so many others were readily imaginable) could bring me on occasion to severe melancholy. Indeed, if I never came truly to despair at the awful arbitrariness of Facts, it was because I never more than notionally accepted them. The *Encyclopedia Tammanica* I read from Aardvaark to Zymurgy in quite the same spirit as I read the *Old School Tales,* my fancy prefacing each entry "Once upon a time . . ." [pp. 80–81]

What really performs the task of hero for Barth is the fable itself. It may not actually redeem us and the university, but it does function as Norman O. Brown tells us all art should function—"to help us find our way back to sources of pleasure that have been rendered inaccessible by the capitulation to the reality-principle which

10. "John Barth: An Interview," p. 6.

we call education or maturity—in other words, to regain the lost laughter of infancy." [11]

The university is an apt image of the waste land not only because it creates the illusion that conceptual knowledge can lead to salvation, but also because it is another of those institutions which our age has come to view as the enemy. It too seizes control over man's life. The campus demonstrations in the late sixties indicate, at least, that students have seen the university as a representative institution, so that revolt against the university is revolt against the system. For the students the contest is just as Barth sees it—a contest to make clear the limited value of learning, to live a life instead of making a transcript, and to have some say about that life, rather than leaving it to a mystery named "Administration." Ultimately, it may be human limitation itself that gives rise to the mystery of fact, which in turn rolls itself into a snowball so large that it overwhelms us as if it were a mysterious external force. But the institution supplies a concrete and immediate image of that mystery; it is something we can struggle against—we can sweat the actual sweat of the hero to measure our hopes of mastery. The university is both the waste land institution and the subtle father who runs our lives in order to teach us how we might best remain children.

Thomas Pynchon's *V.* does not embody its mysterious and malignant forces in an institution, but its heroes are generally passive and Pynchon does not attempt any call to action. Without some institution to contend with, Barth's use of a thematic call to action could possibly have ended in a very dated romanticism, as it does in Ken Kesey's second novel *Sometimes a Great Notion.*

11. Brown, *Life against Death,* p. 60.

Kesey supplies no focus for the forces that oppress Hank Stamper. Stamper does not even have the enemy asylum that McMurphy has in *One Flew over the Cuckoo's Nest,* and so his defiance of what weighs heavy on the human spirit is the kind of romantic posing we would expect from Madison Avenue's "Marlboro Man." Without some focus, some concrete embodiment of the great malignant forces that directly oppose his call to action, Kesey is forced to supply a vague workers' union and a character, Leland Stamper, who represents the institution—the university. Leland talks and minces like the stereotyped anti-intellectual version of an intellectual, and his function in the novel is to learn to be a man, which means unlearn learning and get tough. When Leland makes progress it is announced as the coming of manhood. "You know what's happening? You see what's comin' over him. He's getting the *call.* He's learnin' the gospel of the *woods.* He's forsakin' all that college stuff and he's finding spiritual rediscovery of Mother Nature." [12] The nineteenth-century ring to this statement runs throughout Kesey's book. *Giles Goat-Boy,* while it is undoubtedly too long and sometimes tediously witty, does devise a valid set of metaphors to present human conflicts. *Sometimes a Great Notion* only fills us with a nostalgia for certain sureties we know are no longer available to us. For one thing, the romantic distinction between the campus world and the "real world" no longer works, if only because we no longer have the temerity to insist on one version of the world as the real world. The call to action remains a workable theme only so long as the author resists telling us what that action should be. Once again, the symbolic affirmation that transcends conflicts with-

12. *Sometimes a Great Notion,* p. 221.

out offering a program of action is just about the only affirmative ending the novel of the sixties can have without running into sociology or romanticism.

Although a great many other novelists in the sixties have used the university as setting, they have not made it as organic a part of their overall impact as Barth has. In *A New Life,* for example, Bernard Malamud uses a university setting, but it never becomes more than a setting. His hero, S. Levin, could as well have learned his existential lessons against the backdrop of a counting-house or a sea-going tuna boat. Still others have fallen into the traditional pattern of the "College Novel" as John O. Lyons describes it: "The novel which treats the undergraduate tends to have its hero reject the academy as *merely* a world of ideas, although these ideas are seldom well presented. The novel which treats faculty life tends to turn into a kind of soap opera or a romp through the professional frailties." [13] *The Higher Animals* by H. E. F. Donohue is one example of the latter category; *The Sophomore* by Barry Spacks and *Been Down So Long It Looks Like Up to Me* by Richard Fariña are examples of the former which (when souped-up with narcotics and a certain look-what-a-wild-and-funny-and-lost-kind-of-guy-I-am attitude) seems at present to be the most popular. All of these novels suffer from romanticizing "that world out there where real people live," and from the indiscriminate abuse of "this university life that dries one up." They seem to be set pieces with predictable events, and worst of all, they are vitiated by the very thing they abhor—overintellectualization. The characters these authors create suffer in literary allusions and are never far from a well-turned articulation. It is as if

13. *The College Novel in America* (Carbondale, Ill.: Southern Illinois Univ. Press, 1962), p. 134.

the university were constantly looking over their shoulders making its presence felt in a way far more profound than their thematic anti-academy whine. Barth does not fall into so simple a trap; even though he too is guilty of some overintellectualization, his organic use of the university as a metaphor for the human condition makes his failures and his guilt one more proof that his terms are valid.

In 1964 Leslie Fiedler announced: "It is the revolt against school, and in particular against the university, which most clearly distinguishes the generation of the Sixties from those which immediately preceded it. Given the opportunity, that generation prefers (theoretically at least) to go on the road rather than into school; and even, if forced so far, would choose the madhouse over college, prison over the campus." [14] In view of campus unrest in the late sixties, the urge to desert the university is as yet more theoretical than Mr. Fiedler supposed. The use of the institution as an image of the waste land, and of the university as a particular threat to man's mastery over himself may have just begun to make its impact.

14. *Waiting for the End,* p. 138.

4: THE GRAIL KNIGHT DEPARTS

If the decade of the sixties has produced a significant rebellion against the university as institution, it has, even more clearly, established a protest against the institution of war. We have all known for some time that war is hell; in the past we have coupled that insight with a certain zest for the worst, glorying somewhat covertly in the suffering that has made us a nation of *real men*—men to be reckoned with. The novels which this ambivalent attitude has produced, at best, destroy the illusion that war is always a stimulation for heroic action, but they often mire in some of the questions that have become vital in the 1960s—who runs the war and why? and is it ever really moral, manly, or heroic to be a good modern warrior?

Joseph Heller's *Catch-22* deals with more than the lusty evils of battle; it is a book written for a decade of readers who have been warned about the dangers of the military-industrial complex. It too strikes back at an institution that usurps man's power over his own life, an institution that is a pure threat to the basic maintenance of life. The enemy in Heller's book is not simply the chaos of war, but also the deadly inhuman bureaucracy of the military-economic establishment which claims to be a stay against chaos while it threatens human life more insidiously than battle itself. "The enemy is anybody who's going to get you killed, no matter *which* side he's on." [1] Heller finds it confusing and difficult always to condemn the act of war—to say it was evil to fight against Hitler—but he is unqualified in his condemnation of the military institution that springs from the necessities of battle. The establishment that runs the war goes so far to destroy sanity and life and the human spirit that Heller finds war's greatest evil is its responsibility for the production of organized military inhumanity. *Catch-22* does not really deal with the chaos of war—although that is its persistent backdrop. The emphasis is never on battle, and even the antiwar theme is soft-pedaled when the question of relative morality involves choosing between life-negating war or life-negating bureaucracy. Heller deals instead with one real terror that haunts the novel of the sixties—the organized institution which in the name of reason, patriotism, and righteousness has seized control over man's life. In the novel of the fifties, chaos of any kind provoked our greatest terror—in Bellow, Ellison, or Styron chaos always signified the breakdown of the human spirit in the face of an orderless world. But we seem to have learned that chaos can be faced and our humanity still asserted. In the sixties, the greater terror is provided by the organized institution which has usurped our right to face chaos and to discover our own order and our own humanity—for the institution has provided a surer death of the spirit in the guise of a rational order that lulls us into the long sleep of all that should be human.

1. *Catch-22*, p. 127. Page numbers for all further citations will be included parenthetically in the text.

Catch-22 is certainly not the best book written in the sixties. While many of its problems—repetition, structural looseness, a poorly integrated ending—are explainable, the overall impact of the book is not so impressive as, say, Elkin's *A Bad Man* or Pynchon's *V*. Heller's book is, however, extremely representative and a good basis for summary of the themes, attitudes, devices, and preoccupations of the novel of the sixties. It demonstrates that the single vital quest of the sixties is for the discovery of some way to affirm life against the forces of negation without violating what is human; it faces a world gone mad, where fact and fiction are not distinguishable; it confronts the mystery of fact, a mystery concealing at its heart forces that have seized control over man's life; it finds laughter and the purely symbolic gesture necessary as the only means of handling all these negative forces; it makes clear two themes implicit in the works we have discussed, and important in the chapters to come: the fear that man is regressing toward the inert or inanimate, and the fear that the power which rules us is really some inexplicable, abstract Conspiracy.

The waste land created on the island of Pianosa by the combination of war, the military, and the system of economic free enterprise forces Heller's main character, Yossarian, to become a reluctant Grail Knight. But in a world grown mad, he can only redeem, or more accurately, preserve himself—like Tiresias, like Barth's George Giles, Yossarian is both Fisher King and Grail Knight, wounded loser and hopeful quester. Of all Heller's characters only Yossarian recognizes he is wounded, and only he is really willing to act to save himself. Unlike Kesey's McMurphy, whose salvation comes from heroic confrontation with the waste land institution, or Elkin's Feldman, who despite all morality is

saved by heroic self-affirmation, Heller's Yossarian can be
saved only by a kind of heroic departure. It is perhaps
the final alternative in the gamut of reactions to the institution and to the waste land.

Heller's waste land is defined first by the illogical
idiocies of the Military institution, which claims to exist
in order to deal with the chaos of war, but seems totally
incapable of recognizing what chaos is. The military
commanders constantly lose sight of the simple fact that
they are supposed to beat the enemy; instead they direct
their inverted energies toward self-seeking and an assort-
ment of myopic goals. General Peckem wants to show up
General Dreedle and get his job; Colonel Cathcart wants
"feathers in his cap"; Doc Daneeka wants the European
war to go on so he will not have to go to the unhealthy
climate of the Pacific; and Lieutenant Scheisskopf—ultimately the general in charge of the entire operation, who
proves, as his name implies, that the shitheads are always
in charge—Lieutenant or Commanding General Scheisskopf is totally unaware of anything but parades. The
war is run by ex-Pfc. Wintergreen, a mail clerk, whose
main interests are profit and unprolix prose.

In conjunction with the military machine is the economic system which develops under Milo Minderbinder.
Milo's voracious free enterprise, M&M Enterprises, also
inverts human energy and human action. Milo begins
by supplying exotic foods to the mess halls, but ends by
stressing business deals above the war and the people he
is supposed to serve. His wealth, influence, and sphere of
action become enormous, until he and his profit-seeking
are omnipotent and omnipresent. For business purposes
he takes gas pellets from life jackets and morphine from
first aid kits, leaving the drowning and the wounded
without aid, but with the comforting message that

"what's good for M&M Enterprises is good for the country." The ultimate inversion comes when Milo bombs and strafes his own camp for the Germans, who pay their bills more promptly than some, and kills many Americans at an enormous profit. In the face of criticism, he reveals the overwhelming virtue of his profit and suggests that private industry take over the war so that other individuals will be encouraged to bomb their own men and planes when it is good for business. It is Milo's enterprise that helps keep the men trapped in the waste land; while they languish, he profits; while they clamor to go home, he has them fly his missions; while they die, he expands. "April has been the best month of all for Milo. Lilacs bloomed in April and fruit ripened on the vine. Heartbeats quickened and old appetites were renewed" (p. 257). All of which is good for business. If the wastelanders are trapped in an inverted world, their stirrings mean not that life blooms but that Milo profits.

In the end Milo merges with ex-Pfc. Wintergreen, and Scheisskopf becomes Commanding General. The Military-economic institution rules, and the result is profit for some, but meaningless, inhuman, inane parades for everyone else. This complex institution is so many removes from the war itself that even the weak justifications for war do not justify its existence—it is a totally irrelevant and bureaucratic power that either tosses man to his death or stamps out his spirit. Thus Yossarian has only three alternatives: he can be food for the cannon; he can make a deal with the system; or he can depart, deserting not the war with its implications of preserving political freedom, but abandoning a waste land, a dehumanized, inverted, military-economic machine. Because Heller has emphasized the discontinuity between the military-economic complex and the actual war against

Nazism, Yossarian's desertion can be accepted more easily. The war is not only nearly over, but staying with the machine obviously does not mean fighting the war.

The power of this military-economic machine is best made clear in the mysterious regulation called Catch-22. Catch-22 is the principle used by people in power to justify their illogical use of power. When Yossarian wants to be grounded he cannot be, because only insane people can be grounded, and since only a crazy man would want to fly in war, only those who want to fly must be crazy and can be grounded—those who want to be grounded are sane and must fly. If one of those crazy fliers who could be grounded were to come and ask to be grounded he would be denied because he was sane enough to ask. Catch-22 is the principle that informs the military-economic machine, giving it power and making war possible in the first place. It is the law that says what it commands is right because it is commanded, and the illogical must be done because the command says it is logical. Catch-22 is the untouchable power that has usurped man's control over his own life and handed it over to an institution which manufactures fatal and incredible death traps. Heller gives us the feeling that this power could possibly be beyond even the institution that uses it. It is an abstraction that can be evoked any time we find man subjugated to the absurd—it is the reason, we would be told, for his subjugation. "Catch-22 did not exist, he was positive of that, but it made no difference. What did matter was that everyone thought it existed, and that was much worse, for there was no object or text to ridicule or refute, to accuse, criticize, attack, amend, hate, revile, spit at, rip to shreds, trample upon or burn up" (p. 418). Anyone could be forced into anything, and some insane voice of sanity could always say the reason was Catch-22. But Yossarian can escape it by escaping the military-economic institution, for the officials of that institution are the only ones who use it. Later in this discussion and particularly in later chapters we will see what happens when Catch-22, or something like it, usurps man's life without any visible institution to blame—it becomes a malignant principle, not quite so dignified as the Greek Fates, but rather a mysterious Conspiracy preying upon our paranoia.

Heller's waste land is not just a world of inverted energies; it is a place where insanity reigns and there can be no distinction between fact and fiction. "Insanity is contagious," Yossarian yells, for when he contemplates everyone around him he finds that "everywhere he looked was a nut, and it was all a sensible young man like himself could do to maintain his perspective amid so much madness" (p. 21). But everyone knows, and we are repeatedly told, that Yossarian is really crazy. "That crazy bastard may be the only sane one left" (p. 114). Even a psychiatrist pronounces Yossarian crazy because "he has no respect for excessive authority or obsolete traditions." However, the psychiatrist, suffering from a late puberty, has his own identity problems and so discharges another man in Yossarian's place. Who in the whole novel could be called normal? Major Major Major Major is only in his office to see people when he is out; Colonel Cathcart lives in a world of "black eyes" and "feathers in his cap"; Dunbar wants to be bored so life will be longer; Appleby is crazy enough to love combat; and worst of all, Aarfy, a navigator who cannot find his way, becomes the norm, because he is incapable of comprehending war or human suffering—he is the solid citizen, perfectly complacent, unmoved, and unblamed even as he rapes and murders a serving girl, who is only a serving girl and not even American. Even without war the military-economic bureaucracy drives men mad, and we all echo Chaplain Tappman: "So many monstrous events were occurring that he was no longer positive which events *were* monstrous and which *were* really taking place" (p. 287).

So it is with the whole novel; not only do we question everyone's sanity, but we wonder over the plausibility of almost all the novel's events. Yet, could something so insane as Captain Black's patriotic crusade to prove Major Major Major Major unloyal by forcing everyone to sign dozens of loyalty oaths, while preventing the Major from signing because he is obviously unloyal—could such a crusade really be implausible after we have seen Joseph McCarthy in action? [2] Heller's fiction plays so much with the recognizable that again, as in other novels of the sixties, we wonder if those events that are not recognizable are really just unknown to us and not implausible. Everyone who has been in the army knows "Gus and Wes," the medics who are incompetent; or Pfc. Wintergreen, the low-ranking enlisted man who really runs everything. Heller fills his book with old clichéd army jokes—you are American officers, no other officers can make that statement—and these jokes do give us contact with the ordinary and the recognizable. But old army jokes can turn to horror just as McWatt's game with airplane buzzing finally slices Kid Samson in half, and just as the joke of Huple's cat on Hungry Joe's face becomes a very unfunny death. Black humor is not all that

2. It is clear, of course, that the novel of the sixties takes its legacy as much from the events of the fifties as from World War II —just as the novel of the seventies will surely call upon the *turmoil* of the sixties, even though it will probably turn away from the *novel* of the sixties.

is involved in the abrupt shifts from laughter to pain, for in many cases they are also shifts from the recognizable to the strange, making us aware that fact and fiction are hardly distinguishable. When Yossarian sees a man beating a dog, near the very end of the book, and is reminded of Raskolnikov's dream in *Crime and Punishment*, we are made aware that what was a dream in Raskolnikov's world is a fact in Yossarian's.

The ugliest insanity in the book is the military-economic institution's idea of justice. It too turns the world into a debilitating, valueless waste land. Clevinger, faced with a trial for some response unliked by the arbitrary military gods, is told: "Justice is a knee in the gut from the floor on the chin at night sneaky with a knife brought up down on the magazine of a battleship sandbagged underhanded in the dark without a warning. Garroting. That's what justice is" (p. 82). His trial, along with the later interrogation of the Chaplain, shows that justice is like Catch-22—the defendant is guilty or the military would never have accused him; the accusation is substance enough to prove guilt. It is the military-economic institution, Clevinger's own national bureaucracy and not the enemy, that embodies the power of hate and unjust human destruction. Clevinger learns this as he scrutinizes his judges.

> These three men who hated him spoke his language and wore his uniform, but he saw their loveless faces set immutable into cramped, mean lines of hostility and understood instantly that nowhere in the world, not in all the fascist tanks or planes or submarines, not in the bunkers behind the machine guns or mortars or behind the blowing flame throwers, not even among all the expert gunners of the crack Hermann Goering

Anti-aircraft Division or among the grisly connivers in all the beer halls in Munich and everywhere else, were there men who hated him more. [p. 83]

When Yossarian cranks this vision up a notch to deal with divine justice, he finds God has created a lousy world filled with unnecessary suffering. He and his friends try to parcel out justice with at least some accuracy, giving malaria to the man who deserves it, money to the man who worked for it, and a dose of clap to the man who earned it. Left to God, these varied visitations had been scrambled unjustly. The subject is not pursued, but we are left to understand that God, even for those who do not believe in Him, most likely employs Catch-22 in His dealings with man.

Even though Colonel Cathcart and Milo Minderbinder initiate both petty and large-scale injustices, they neither get their just deserts nor become the particular targets of hate and blame. As pervasive as Catch-22 is, so is man's injustice to man. War and the military-economic institution perpetuate a waste land, generation after generation, creating an endless cycle of victims and victimizers, hopeful Grail Knights and wounded Fisher Kings. Cathcart, too, must have been a sometime victim. Near the end of the book, Yossarian is saddled with Nately's Whore who pops out of every bush and around every corner to attack him because of Nately's death. However guiltless Yossarian may be of that one death, he is not guiltless—he has suffered as a victim, but has also been a victimizer. So Nately's Whore will follow him forever, a kind of universal principle reminding him that he will always be unjustly beset and will probably always deserve it. Yossarian understands his burden and even accepts it, saying of Nately's Whore:

She and everyone younger had every right to blame
him and everyone older for every unnatural tragedy
that befell them; just as she, even in her grief, was to
blame for every man-made misery that landed on her
kid sister and on all other children behind her. Someone had to do something. Every victim was a culprit,
every culprit a victim, and somebody had to stand up
sometime to try to break the lousy chain of inherited
habit that was imperiling them all. [p. 414]

The real power that victimizes us is our own perpetual
Catch-22. Yossarian attempts to break the chain in the
end when he hunts for the Whore's kid sister to take
with him on his departure. Perhaps, as Heller sees it, a
recognition of this useless, generation-after-generation,
self-imposed cycle will open a real "generation gap" and
cause someone to refuse the usual inheritance of habit.

The military-economic institution is characterized also
by the same kind of meaningless aspiration that plagued
Barth's university waste land. If Colonel Cathcart did
not want so badly to be a general, to get an A on his
transcript, his pilots might not have gotten trapped in
his escalating demands. All touch with what should be
the purpose of Cathcart's command is lost as aspiration
itself becomes the final end. And why does Cathcart want
to be a general? asks Lieutenant-colonel Korn. "For the
same reason I want to be a colonel. What else have we
got to do? Everyone teaches us to aspire to higher things.
A general is higher than a colonel and a colonel is higher
than a lieutenant colonel. So we're both aspiring" (p.
435). That way goes what is left of the American Dream.
Meanwhile Cathcart's aspirations, coupled with Milo's
supply-and-demand compulsions, Peckem's self-aggran-
dizement, and Scheisskopf's dream of better and better

parades turns Pianosa into a waste land where no value exists except some vague idea of advancement. A great deal of Heller's comic awfulness comes from showing how everyone loses sight of the war itself, shuffling it like a minor report beneath the weight of military and economic aspirations.

Perhaps the most frightening characteristic of this waste land is the way the military-economic institution deprives the individual of any humanity and leads him insistently toward the inanimate and inert. It is not a simple matter of denying a man's identity, although that is done too, but the virtual destruction of anything that makes a man a live human being. The company records show that Doc Daneeka is dead, and even while he stands yelling that he lives, he is removed from pay records, chow records, and PX privileges. His wife collects insurance, grows rich, receives sympathetic notification: "Dear Mrs., Mr., Miss, or Mr. and Mrs. Daneeka: Words cannot express the deep personal grief I experienced when your husband, son, father or brother was killed, wounded or reported missing in action" (p. 354). She moves, leaving no forwarding address, and Doc Daneeka perches like a vulture on a friend's campstool, dead to the army and dead in every sense but the physical. No bullet could have done a better job. People are continually treated like things, not by the enemy who is out to kill them, but by their own military establishment. Scheisskopf, in his restless quest for better parades,

considered every means of improvement, even nailing the twelve men in each rank to a long two-by-four beam of seasoned oak to keep them in line. The plan was not feasible, for making a ninety-degree turn would have been impossible without nickel-alloy swivels in-

serted in the small of every man's back, and Lieutenant
Scheisskopf was not sanguine at all about obtaining
that many nickel-alloy swivels from Quartermaster or
enlisting the cooperation of the surgeons at the hospital. [p. 74–75]

The men are government issue like a bedpan or a gear,
as Yossarian is told. There is no value or dignity in human life; thus Aarfy, Lieutenant Aardvaark, is the perfect
symbol of the inhuman man. He is like "a sack of in-
flated rubber," or "an eerie ogre in a dream." He stands
over Yossarian's narrow crawlway in the bombardier's
section of their aircraft, stuffing space with his fat, but
maddeningly unable to recognize another man's pain.
Aarfy is exactly what the military-economic institution
condones. His rape and murder of Michaela go unpunished, while Yossarian is picked up for being AWOL.
Aarfy's horrible act is symbolic of every inhumane dismemberment and every death ever caused by the complacent and the self-righteous, by those who have been
turned into artifacts of the system and cannot comprehend how any other artifact could possibly have feelings,
could possibly suffer. But Heller wants us to know man
is not an object. Yossarian learns the secret of humanity
from the dying Snowden who spills out his guts—man
can be garbage; we must assert the spirit to make him
otherwise.
     The end product of the military-economic waste land
is the perfectly inanimate, inert man—"the soldier in
white." He strikes a terrible fear in everyone's heart, and
rightly so, for in him Dunbar, Yossarian, and all the
hospital patients see the image of their future. The waste
land can dehumanize no further:

The soldier in white was encased from head to toe in plaster and gauze. He had two useless legs and two useless arms . . . the two strange legs hoisted from the hips, the two strange arms anchored up perpendicularly, all four limbs pinioned strangely in air by lead weights suspended darkly above him that never moved. Sewn into the bandages over the insides of both elbows were zippered lips through which he was fed clear fluid from a clear jar. A silent zinc pipe rose from the cement on his groin and was coupled to a slim rubber hose that carried waste from his kidneys and dripped it efficiently into a clear, stoppered jar on the floor. When the jar on the floor was full, the jar feeding his elbow was empty, and the two were simply switched quickly so that stuff could drip back into him. All they ever really saw of the soldier in white was a frayed black hole over his mouth. [p. 10]

As an act of human compassion, the nurses polish his zinc and scrub his plaster, but when he dies it takes a little while before anyone notices.

The more power an institution has over the individual the less control he has over his own life and the less he is able to act. Fear of becoming inanimate is an increasingly persistent theme in the novel of the sixties as the ruling powers, the waste land makers, become more and more abstract. When an asylum or a jail or a university rules man, the hero is able to act and strike out at a concrete target as does McMurphy in *One Flew over the Cuckoo's Nest,* or Feldman in *A Bad Man,* or even George Giles in *Giles Goat-Boy.* But when the enemy shifts between being a concrete military-economic institution and a broad abstraction like Catch-22, then the hero finds himself in a more subtle trap. In Heller's waste land the only possible affirmative response in the face of powers that threaten death or conversion to the inanimate is to depart for the sake of life. This may be affirmative, but it is also the very last action a man can take. And, as an alternative it puts us one step closer to Eliot's inert Tiresias and to the passive hero who has lost power over his life to something so vague he can only call it a conspiracy. Yossarian prepares us for the passive hero, enervated by fear and paranoia, moving toward the living inert and wishing he could believe that conspiracies made no sense—even though they are there. "They're trying to kill me," Yossarian tells Clevinger, who wishes to know who "They" are. "Everyone of them. . . . As far back as Yossarian could recall, he explained to Clevinger with a patient smile, somebody was always hatching a plot to kill him" (p. 20). If the military-economic institution can make us all soldiers in white, what can *They* do—They who can be neither seen nor named. As we shall see, especially in the discussion of Thomas Pynchon, the fear of conspiracy in the novel of the sixties begins as a joke, like everything else, but ends as a decidedly confusing possibility. After all, They *are* trying to kill Yossarian.

It is clear that under the domination of the military-economic institution and the mystery of Catch-22, Heller's waste land has all the characteristics we have found to be typical. All energies are inverted and result in death and destruction instead of love, fulfillment, or renewal. The men alternate between making war and making Italian whores, but even Yossarian's "loves" are as "unholy" as any of Eliot's tired Belladonnas, including his pathetic typist with her clerk. The men are frazzled wastelanders, characterized by an enervating and neu-

rotic pettiness that culminates in Hungry Joe's nightmares; they are divided by guilts, particularly over the
value of their war efforts; they are alienated, aimless,
and bored. They long for escape and even death—almost everyone does either die or disappear. They are
close to being inert and are helpless in the face of a total
disintegration of values. Life constantly leads to a reduction of all human dignity or measures man in terms of
his mercantile worth—as Milo puts it, "a thousand dollars ain't such a bad price for a medium bomber and
crew." They are spiritually debilitated and the Chaplain
cannot help; they are physically debilitated and the
medics simply paint them violet. Only Yossarian is sane
enough to recognize he is wounded by the waste land he
lives in, and only Yossarian is crazy enough to become a
Grail Knight in search of some way to stay alive and still
assert his humanity.

Yossarian sits somewhat uneasily on the Grail Knight's
white horse, especially in the early part of the book, but
he does undergo some education that redirects his continued devotion to staying alive. In the beginning he is
selfish, but not as Milo or Doc Daneeka or even Colonel
Cathcart is selfish. He wants nothing but to live. With
the exception of his friend Orr, who supplies the ultimate alternative, Yossarian is the only wastelander who
actively tries to do something to save himself. He makes
his pilot turn back from doom-threatening Bologna, he
moves the bomb line when everyone else can only watch
it, he refuses to fly, goes naked, walks backward. And
everything he tries is, of course, futile. Meanwhile, Heller
shifts the moral emphasis of the book, allowing Yossarian some conscience and burying our objection that
Yossarian lets others die so he can live. Yossarian has
done his share in the war and even more; Heller wants

the emphasis not on his morality, but on his great and necessary will to live. On the other hand, Heller continues to take moral potshots at the absurd patriotism which makes us kill and be killed for some abstraction called country. He rigs a series of conversations between an old wise Italian whoremaster and a young propaganda-fed American so that a few statements can be made about the foolishness of man's pride in war, and the idiocy of his inhumanity. Then, turning about again, at the very end, Heller has Yossarian justify his morality with a touch of that same evil pride in nationalism that Heller has condemned: "I earned that medal I got, no matter what their reasons for giving it to me. I've flown seventy goddamn combat missions. Don't talk to me about fighting to save my country. I've been fighting all along to save my country. Now I'm going to fight a little to save myself. The country's not in danger any more, but I am!" (p. 455).

Clearly, we are ultimately supposed to put aside moral considerations and embrace Yossarian for his affirmation of life and for his defiance of the military-economic machine. If he stays to fight, he fights only for the greedy Cathcart and the wolfish Milo Minderbinder. We certainly can accept Yossarian entirely on the basis of his will to live, but if Heller wants us to set moral considerations aside, or to see war as immoral so that we will not morally judge Yossarian for not wanting to fight, then he has fudged his issue. Fudged it, because he apologizes for Yossarian by making him call to our attention that he has been a good fighter; he has already fulfilled his moral contract. We are, in effect, prevented from forming a clear idea of the morality of the war, and we are prevented from setting moral considerations aside to judge Yossarian entirely on his will to live. Stanley

Elkin made us love and accept Feldman in *A Bad Man* by showing us great vitality without every excusing his morality. Only by that kind of insistence can an author convince us that the question of life over death transcends all other questions, moral and otherwise; and that, I believe, is what Heller intended to do.

Yossarian's education in his quest for life really reaches its culmination when he makes his night trip through the eternal city of Rome. The trip is the Grail Knight's approach to the Chapel Perilous and it decidedly echoes Eliot's eerie inverted setting. Yossarian discovers the pervasiveness of human insanity: "Nothing warped seemed bizzare anymore in his strange, distorted surroundings." He stumbles across the intense poverty of thin-legged children and coarsened mothers; the convulsions of an ailing soldier who is picked up and put down like a rag doll by other men impotent to really help; eerie sounds of snow being shoveled and of people crying out variations on a plea for help; a man beating a dog while people watch; and a man beating a boy while people watch. Assaulted on all sides, Yossarian, the Grail Knight, "thought he knew how Christ must have felt as he walked through the world, like a psychiatrist through a ward full of nuts, like a victim through a prison full of thieves" (p. 424). When he tries to escape, Yossarian encounters two final Eliot-like effects. He finds himself walking on a litter of human teeth, cluttering his path like debris; and he watches a man arrested by the police for no reason crying out, "Help Police Help," as a warning not a summons—then he sees the man's face go white with fear, his eyes pulsating, "flapping like bat's wings." The bat wings should recall the final approach to Eliot's Chapel Perilous; but instead of a flash of lightning, Yossarian comes across the most horrible inhumanity of the book—Aarfy's brutal, unpunished murder of Michaela, the serving girl. Instead of the voice of the Thunder telling Yossarian to give, sympathize, and control, he hears the voice of the military, cold and inhuman, as the MPs carry him off. "Their marching footsteps on the dull tile floor thundered like an awesome, quickening drum roll" (p. 430). It is a moment of epiphany in the novel, incorporating in a single symbol much of Heller's statement and much of the entire novel's warning —that in the place of the humane, in the place of the Thunder preaching compassion, we find the thunder of the marching boot, the destruction of the human, arrested by the growth of the military-economic institution. We should have been prepared; Yossarian's approach to the Chapel Perilous was marked by "a frigid fine rain," not the rain of fertility but the inverted rain of destruction.

Yossarian, however, is initiated in this scene because it does lead to the healing of his own wound. On the other hand, it also prepares us for the realization that Yossarian can save only himself—there is no possibility of redeeming this waste land. When pitted against the powers of the military-economic institution, the power of an individual man is at its peak if that man can gain control of his own life. Yossarian, as Grail Knight, undergoes one further temptation. Colonel Korn offers him an odious deal that would make him a part of the whole system; but his memory of Snowden's message—man is garbage without the spirit—coupled with an apparition that comes to warn him nightly, dissuades Yossarian from selling his soul and losing his humanity. The novel progresses toward its ending through a very academic discussion between Yossarian and ex-college professor Danby. They check off all of man's alternatives in a waste land ruled by the military-economic institution and by Catch-22. Everything leads to death, to the inanimate, or to the betrayal of humanity. They conclude that there are no alternatives; man's life is hopeless. Then they hear about Orr—what better name for an alternative—who was supposed to have been shot down. Instead, he has gone to Sweden; he had practiced crash landings, cultivated a look of innocence and idiocy, and acted to preserve his life. For a brief moment we wonder how many of the characters in the book who "disappeared" really found sanctuary just by getting out from under the institution. What might have happened to Dunbar, to Clevinger, to Major Major Major Major, to Major _____ de Coverley, and to all the disappeared Italian whores? Yossarian decides to go to Sweden and answers Danby's objections: his decision is not negative or escapist, " 'I'm not running *away* from my responsibilities. I'm running *to* them. There's nothing negative about running away to save my life' " (p. 461).

Yossarian's choice is meant to prove that no matter what else a man does he must find a way to affirm life over death. But, happily for the novel, the alternative is not a concrete proposal for universal human action, as some critics have taken it to be. We need not all literally go to Sweden. Heller's ending is like many other endings in the novel of the sixties; its affirmation is possible only through a symbolic gesture. What is important to Heller is that man need not be beaten—the choices may be extreme, and like Yossarian, man may always be plagued by Nately's Whore, something popping up everywhere to threaten life; but still, life is possible and man can always find some way to assert the human spirit. There is something undeniably bleak about an alternative which leads the Grail Knight to depart from the waste land in order to survive, especially when we consider our long tradition of employing the pattern of withdrawal and return. But Heller's fable of madness makes it very clear that any grander plan, any hope that an individual redeemer, a super-Yossarian, can return to benefit all men is as black a joke as the cat on Hungry Joe's face.

Taken a step further, the departure of the Grail Knight could also mean he has been defeated, that he departs not to affirm life but to survive as a dispossessed man. This is, of course, a negative response in which there is no hope of redemption for either the individual or the waste land. Jerome Charyn's fine book *On the Darkening Green,* does, indeed, present such a darkening vision in which the hero departs because he is beaten. The word *dispossessed* rings repeatedly throughout the book, and Charyn's major character, Nick Lapucci, is dispossessed of his family, of his home, and finally of his only effort to be a Grail Knight. The setting for most of the book is an institution—the "Blattenburg Home and School for Wayward Jewish Boys"—but the larger background is meant to be the war. The Home is a microcosm that reveals the inhumane causes and effects of war. The boys in the Home are all dispossessed, rejects from society. They are badly abused and taught only the ethics of war. The climax of the book comes when Nick attempts to assist a group of the young boys to rebel against the system. Nick is usually passive, but on this one occasion he asks himself if it is possible to "rout the jailer," to be "the new knight of the realm." He fails and is forced to leave—later we find that everyone's position has worsened. The failure of the oppressed to halt oppression in the Boy's Home is paralleled at the end of the book by a failed race riot in New York, and that in turn parallels the widest symbol of man's oppressive inhumanity, the failure that results in war. Like Heller, Charyn shows us we are trapped in a cycle of victims and victimizers, the oppressed and the oppressors, but the power of the individual to break the cycle is so far shrunk in Charyn's vision that defeat on every level seems inevitable. In his second novel, *Going to Jerusalem,* Hope is a woman closely identified with Eliot's neurotic speaker in "A Game of Chess." The book is structured around chess tournaments, and the major character, red-bearded Ivan, is an epileptic, a beaten Fisher King, who is all the more beaten because he attempts to be a human being who cares. For Charyn, knowing the condition of the world, as one of his characters in *On the Darkening Green* tells us, is to be "sitting on a pile of shit."

With the knowledge that we have not exhausted the novelist's response to the institution, we can use the departure of the Grail Knight as a conveniently symbolic point to move on and consider a different set of responses to the dilemmas we have already noted as central to the novel of the sixties. When the power that controls man's life becomes something larger and more abstract than the institution, as both Heller and Charyn intimate, the power of the individual shrinks and he can no longer be a Grail Knight even to himself. In that sense, many novelists in the sixties feel that the potency represented by the Grail Knight has truly departed. Thus, they shift the focus of their books to seek an understanding of the waste land and the power that rules it. " 'Who can believe in God today?' " one of Charyn's characters in *On the Darkening Green* asks, " 'Only lunatics! But devils? That's another story. The devils are in charge of the world. Who else could bring about so much madness in

such an organized way?' " (p. 164). If it is the devil who
has power over us and who turns our world into a waste
land—if it is the devil who is behind organized madness
—then, for the novelist of the sixties, the devil is Conspiracy.

PART II: THE WASTE LAND AS CONSPIRACY

The waste land is a world in which spiritual values have decayed because there is no mythology to embody a supreme being, and so no proper object for man's spiritual longings. But the impulse toward belief in a superior being, the desire for a spiritually higher existence—twisted, as we have seen, into aspiration for an A on the transcript—has not died. A great many novels written in the sixties deal with what has happened to this impulse; the problem is not unique, but perhaps the response is. When a man of the sixties feels he has lost control of his own life, when he thinks no single individual can influence large public events, when he feels he can no longer cope with the irrationality of public and private affairs, when he yearns for some transcendent explanation and meaning, he begins to find patterns in the accidents of fortune—mysteries in the indifference of fact. Or, perhaps, he does discover the devil. Nothing better indicates how intractable our waste land has grown than the inversion of our spiritual longings to a fearful belief in the absolute malicious force of Conspiracy. Many novelists in the sixties have recognized that the fear of Conspiracy is a serious business, and that as a substitute for spiritual faith it has become our peculiar contribution to the landscape of the waste land.

Unseen and unknowable, Conspiracy is a far more frightening force to contend with than the Institution. But it may also seem a better explanation for the organized insanity of the nuclear age. Speculation on the loss of the individual's control over his own life has become so widespread that we are even getting confessions from the American political world and the popular public media. In a *New York Times* editorial intended to urge that we grapple with our problems anew, James Reston reluctantly admitted in 1969: "In the vast disorder of human affairs today—private and public—something new is beginning to drift into the American spirit. Other

societies have lived with it for many generations: it is
the element of doubt that in this convulsive and contra-
dictory age we still have the capacity to master our problems."

To many novelists this would be a masterpiece of un-
derstatement, for the novels that deal with the effects of
our belief in Conspiracy are peopled with characters who
are passive, inert, inanimate, who have given up the
struggle to master their own problems. At best they sustain themselves by waiting to understand the true meaning of Conspiracy. For men who feel helpless, Conspiracy
is both Deity and Demon, and such a feeling is far more
widespread than Reston's modest admission would indicate. In May of 1966 *Esquire* ran an article called "Wake
Up, America, It Can Happen Here: A Post-McCarthy
Guide to Twenty-Three Conspiracies by Assorted Enemies Within." It is easy to laugh at some of these twenty-
three representative conspiracies—The Mental Health
Conspiracy, The Flag-Stamp Intrigue, The Zip Code
Plot, The Great Blackout Conspiracy, and so on. (The
Flag-Stamp Intrigue and the Zip Code Plot sound like
something created by Thomas Pynchon for *The Crying
of Lot 49*.) But will the same people who laugh at these
conspiracies laugh at the Kennedy-Assassination Plot, or
the Conspiracy of the Military-Industrial Complex, also
listed among *Esquire*'s twenty-three? The possibility that
we are in the hands of a far-flung Conspiracy provides
excellent material for the black humorist. It is all probably just a joke, probably a product of our national
atomic-age paranoia—but who among us is sure? And
what could be funnier than finding out that some Organization is actually putting time, effort, and energy into
creating such a mess—what could be blacker than the

terror provoked by finding out there are such powerful and efficient mess-makers. Perhaps, in the end, we have to be a little paranoid in order to stay sane in the contemporary world.

5: THE ILLUSION AND THE POSSIBILITY
OF CONSPIRACY

THE ILLUSION

Understanding Thomas Pynchon's mysterious novel *V.*
is like understanding the twentieth century. Pursue V.
and you are like Herbert Stencil, the "century's child,"
born in 1901, buried in the outrageous facts of contemporary experience, and convinced that "events seem to be
ordered in an ominous logic." V. is everything that happens in the twentieth century and everything that might
happen—as if you could clutch a handful of the times
from our atmosphere and tack a letter on it, making it
palpable so it can be poked around and examined, if
not known. Pynchon has attempted to show us the essential qualities of our time. Like a prose version of Eliot's
The Waste Land, V. pictures a world where love and
mythology have failed, and it points out the path we
follow: "The street of the 20th Century, at whose far
end or turning—we hope—is some sense of home or
safety. But no guarantees. A street we are put at the
wrong end of, for reasons best known to the agents who

put us there. If there are agents. But a street we must walk." [1]

In a sense, Pynchon is creating the mystery of Fate itself. For, ultimately, understanding V. is understanding the compulsive direction we take in our headlong plunge down the street of our century. As always with Fate, V. leads us to wonder if we take that plunge because of mysterious forces guiding us, or if the plunge as well as Fate, V., and everything else is the way it is because we are the way we are. For Herbert Stencil, V.'s "emissaries haunt the century's streets." For the more reliable Fausto Maijstral, "There is more accident to it than a man can ever admit to in a lifetime and stay sane." Thus, we have the two poles of Fate, and the essential mystery of V.— either there is some ominous logic to the direction of man's life or life is a series of random accidents defined only by the impulses of the living. In either case, however, the direction of our plunge is clear to Pynchon. Insofar as Fate is knowable, insofar as V. is identifiable, and insofar as our future is predictable, it all points to a "dream of annihilation." V. as woman, V. as war, V. as conspiracy—it all adds up to what old Godolphin discovers about Vheissu in 1898 or what Von Trotha puts into effect in 1904—"Vernichtungs Befehl" (Annihilation Orders). Annihilation is the nightmare of the twentieth century, and it is perhaps our Fate—a possibility brought to our attention in 1945 when young Herbert Stencil begins his quest and the United States drops the Atomic Bomb. The mystery of V. is the mystery of why we pursue our destruction; it is the mystery of fact in the twentieth century, which points repeatedly to the madness of annihilation—not to the hope of love, but to the

1. *V.*, pp. 323–24. Page numbers for all further citations will be included parenthetically in the text.

waste land after the holocaust, to "the desert, or a row of false shop fronts; a slag pile, a forge where the fires are banked, these and the street and the dreamer, only an inconsequential shadow himself in the landscape, partaking of the soullessness of these other masses and shadows; this is the 20th Century nightmare" (p. 324).

V. encompasses three realms, interrelated in a process which attempts to make us understand the essential qualities of our century and the extensiveness of our nightmare. "The process is a part of daily news," Richard Poirier tells us, "and no other novelist predicts and records it with Pynchon's imaginative and stylistic grasp of contemporary materials." [2] The three realms of the novel are the private, the public-political, and what might be called the metaphysical. The private realm evolves from the stories of Benny Profane, Rachel Owlglass, the Whole Sick Crew, and Fausto Maijstral's confessions. The action takes place between December 1955 and September 1956. It ends with Benny Profane running down a Malta street in sudden blackness toward the sea. Abandoned and teamed with Brenda Wigglesworth, the "inviolable Puritan," Benny seems finally at the end of his Street, on the edge of his own "Day of Doom."

The public, political, and international realm includes all the stories that relate to the Lady V. and the events of twentieth-century upheaval:

1898—Egypt; Fashoda; Victoria Wren
1899—Florence; Venezuelan uprising; Plot to steal the *Birth of Venus*; Intimations of World War I; The Vheissu Plot involving Vesuvius, M. Vogt, his spy school, and Victoria Wren
1901—Herbert Stencil's birth; Queen Victoria's death

2. *New York Times,* 1 May 1966, p. 5.

1904—Von Trotha's Vernichtungs Befehl, putting down Black uprising in South West Africa by introducing brutalities surpassed only in World War II

1913—Paris; Intimations of Russian Revolution; Stirrings of World War I; The Lady V. nameless and in love with Melanie l'Heuremaudit; Russia and the Orient linked in a suspected "movement to overthrow Western Civilization"

1918—Evan Godolphin's face ruined; World War I; Inspiration of young Schoenmaker

1919—Death of Sydney Stencil; Malta's June Disturbances; Intimations of World War II and Mussolini; Veronica Manganese

1922—Uprising in South West Africa; Foppl's decadent seige party; Intimations of Hitler; Vera Meroving; Hedwig Vogelsang

1934—Fairing's Parish in New York sewers, with Veronica the rat; Intimations of World War II and possible apocalypse; American Depression

1943—Bombing of Malta in World War II; In Valleta, Malta, the death and dismantling of the Lady V. disguised as the transvestite "Bad Priest"

1945—Beginning of Herbert Stencil's quest; Atomic Bomb

1956—Stencil's abandonment of Malta in pursuit of Mme Viola, an oneiromancer, a diviner of dreams, who might finally reveal the dream of annihilation that Stencil pursues

Other public events are scattered throughout the book as Pynchon keeps us aware of world news, current fashions, and wide-scale catastrophes, natural and otherwise. Herbert Stencil moves in both the private and public realms on his mysterious quest, but Stencil is a third-person object himself, with no real private being. He may be a quester, but he is no Grail Knight—he is as much a schlemiel and a human yo-yo as Benny Profane. He is indeed the century's child, functioning only to help us understand the century, but not as a redeemer. He is not even a seeker of identity, for Pynchon, like other novelists of the sixties, mocks the whole tired idea of an identity search by putting the jargon we have evolved to describe that search into the mouths of the *Time*-Magazine–reading, fashionable decadents called the Whole Sick Crew. Pynchon is not interested in failed redeemers; he is interested in the waste land itself, in the landscape of the twentieth century, the Street which has become, according to Fausto Maijstral, "the Kingdom of Death."

The third realm in the novel deals with the metaphysical, or perhaps ontological, question of whether V. exists as an actual force or only as the fictional heading under which we list the random facts of twentieth-century life. Do the facts of our century's private and public life add up to an actually existing force that has seized control over man's life, or are we constructing a demon to explain why man has lost the power of significant individual action and become a little less human? What better explains the fabulous direction contemporary fact has taken, the mystery of absurdity, and the threat of annihilation —what better explains the loss of man's coveted *virtù* than the existence of some usurping power symbolized, aptly, by the letter V. and meaning not individual excellence, but wide-scale, untouchable, metaphysical Conspiracy? Pynchon's *V.* deals with that same mystery we have seen to be the compelling preoccupation of the novel in the sixties—to requote Benjamin DeMott's words: given the nature of contemporary experience, our worst nightmare is "that events and individuals are unreal, and that power to alter the course of the age, of my life and your life, is actually vested nowhere." [3] *V*. presents a series of visible manifestations in public and private life that hint at a mystery behind everyday fact. As we are told, the Lady V. as well as every other V.-word from the V-Note Bar to Via dei Vecchietti are only "symptoms" of what makes our world a waste land. The symptoms and the V.'s are everywhere (even the color of the hardbound *V*. is violet). The question is: do the symptoms reveal a master cabal still in the making, a universal paranoia, or a world deluded by its need for mystery and meaning, its need to replace a lost mythology? (Even Herbert Stencil admits he may only be driven by something "buried" in him "that needed a mystery.")

As I have mentioned and as I hope to demonstrate, V. is the essential nature of our century, pointing always toward our haunting communal "dream of annihilation"; however, only after we have examined the symptoms and manifestations of that dream, all the public and private appearances of V., can we say in what sense Pynchon feels V. to be an actually existing entity. It is the same question we have seen before—is it possible that deep in the soul of our century we will discover not the American Dream but a dream which proves we ourselves are the source of a waste land world gone mad; or is there really an unknown Master Conspiracy, a Big Bad Wolf? The question itself may sound like ripe material for a joke, and so it is at times, but that only makes it one more example of black humor, of the comic becoming nightmare; the fear of conspiracy is a real fact in contemporary life— it is perhaps the stuff that V.'s are made on.

3. "Looking for Intelligence in Washington," p. 96. These words were italicized in the original.

By using a series of repetitions, verbal echoes, and baf-
fling coincidences, Pynchon interrelates the private, the
public, and the metaphysical realms of his book, and gives
us the sense that V. is omnipresent. Any thing we learn
in any realm contributes toward an overall understanding
of V. What is true about Victoria Wren is true of Vheissu
and helps us understand V., the essential nature of the
twentieth century. The implied sexuality of Esther's nose
operation recalls the sexual nature of Lady V., who is
often a seducer and a saint combined (like Victoria Wren
and Veronica the rat), and that in turn relates to Fina
Mendoza who is the spiritual leader and gang bang for
a New York street gang. The private and public realms
join to point out that abuse of sexuality is one pervasive
symptom of V. and of our century; therefore abuse of
sexuality is one of the things that leads us by steps toward
fulfilling our dream of annihilation. For example: the
sexuality of Esther's nose job is a comic inversion of the
usual joke about men and the length of their noses,
demonstrating a vaguely unhealthy reversal of role playing; the next step, a little less funny, is Mafia Winsome's
tyrannical theory of "Heroic Love," where the woman is
the aggressor; one step further and the reversal of roles
becomes an undeniable inversion when the Lady V. appears as the Bad Priest, a transvestite, who in that role is
finally annihilated. Picking up the events of the book at
any point can lead to what Pynchon repeatedly calls a
"daisy chain" of events, interrelating the private and the
public realms and centering around some one quality of
twentieth-century life.

Pynchon, we come to see, sets up his own version of
correspondences; that is, the private individual does in
microcosm what the public governments do in macrocosm, thereby raising an individual foible to a public,

and perhaps universal, metaphysical principle. Benny
Profane cannot love just as governments cannot get along,
and Rachel tells him, "You've taken your own flabby,
clumsy soul and amplified it into a Universal Principle"
(p. 383). In the same way, Plots come into being. Just as
the individual assigns causes to situations he does not
understand, the government assigns causes on a grand
scale—Presto! we have Causes, Plots, Conspiracies. "People read what news they want to and each accordingly
builds his own rathouse of history's rags and straws. . . .
God knows what is going on in the minds of cabinet min-
isters, heads of state and civil servants in the capitals of
the world. Doubtless their private versions of history show
up in action" (p. 225). While old Godolphin fumbles
with his doubtful stories of Vheissu, perhaps a fictional
place, old Stencil theorizes that Vheissu is a code name
for Venezuela which indicates a plot to take over the
world by invading a subterranean network of tunnels
through volcanoes starting first with Vesuvius. The plot
is revealed by Madame Vogt as she plays her viola da
gamba, and as some real Venezuelans plot the theft of
Botticelli's *Birth of Venus*. Not only have we moved from
the realm of private idiosyncrasy to that of public affairs
(resulting in a riot), but the mysterious V. has multiplied
itself into a metaphysical principle of Plot. We know it
is untrue, as we do of other plots in the novel, but the
point here is that comprehension of private failures leads
by analogy to an understanding of public dilemmas; V.,
the dream of the century, can be approached on any level.
Thus, as we come to understand the characteristics of V.
we recognize the widespread mystery of its existence.
When old Godolphin tells us Vheissu with its rainbow of
colors is a "dream of annihilation," we are prepared to

register this as the essential truth about the colorful Lady V. and V. in general.

The intertwinings of plot and the parallels between different realms in the world of V. not only instruct us in the step-by-step metaphysics of conspiracy, but also make us wonder if in Pynchon's world conspiracies might not sometimes be true. Could all these connections be accident? German names and German characters constantly appear in connection with ominous intimations. Plotters in Egypt 1898 meet in a German beer hall, and so do plotters in 1899 in Florence; Germans are behind the scenes in Paris 1913; Foppl's German castle is the scene of strange machinations in 1922 and Von Trotha's cruelty in 1904 foreshadows World War II. The suggestions are numerous, and every manifestation of V. occurs in connection with some possibility of influence on a real and historical war.

Pynchon also uses coincidence in his fictional plot; not only does Stencil cross the lines from one part of the story to the next, but so do Hugh and Evan Godolphin, Father Fairing, and Fausto Maijstral. The coincidences built into the fictional plot of *V.* reinforce the thematic question of whether things happen by chance or by malicious design. Other kinds of parallels in the book make us aware that Pynchon is focusing on the waste land of the twentieth century rather than trying to characterize certain people: Benny Profane has a theory of Streets and so does Fausto Maijstral; Rachel Owlglass and Rooney Winsome talk of decadence, so do Mondaugen and the director of ballet, M. Itague—the Street and twentieth-century decadence are emphasized, not the characters, whose theories and discussions are almost interchangeable. The traditional device of foreshadowing is used as another kind of parallel between the different realms of the novel: Benny's old dream-joke about the boy with the golden screw in his navel, who removes the screw and loses his ass and all his other parts, warns us of the fate of Lady V., who has a sapphire removed from her naval and is literally disassembled by children on the island of Malta; and it is also another dream of annihilation. There are even verbal echoes that occur periodically in different voices: "the balloon's gone up," "the dance of death," "the world is all that the case is," and "keep cool, but care." Songs appear throughout the book no matter what the setting or who the characters involved. All this complex echoing and interrelating of the private, public, and metaphysical realms, similar to Eliot's method in *The Waste Land,* contributes to the mystery of the book and makes it clear that V. is everything symptomatic of our century and that all the symptoms point toward a communal dream of annihilation.

The two major symptoms of the twentieth century, as both Pynchon and Eliot have described them, are the inversion of love and the inversion of religion. Thus, every public and private appearance of V.—as woman, place, or concept—is connected to these two characteristics. The inversion of love is demonstrated in the abuse of sex and in the continued appearance of war. The inversion of religion appears not only through the distorted beliefs of Father Fairing and Victoria Wren but through the substitution of belief in conspiracy for faith in a supreme Being. If, for example, we were to follow the progressive appearances of the Lady V.—Victoria Wren in 1898 and 1899; V., the lover of Melanie l'Heuremaudit in Paris 1913; Veronica Manganese on Malta in 1919; Vera Meroving and her accomplice Hedwig Vogelsang in South West Africa in 1922; and the Bad Priest in Valletta,

Malta 1943—if we were to scrutinize these appearances of one kind of V., we would find in each case the inversion of love in transvestitism, fetishism, lesbianism, or simple exploitation; we would find the intimation of one of our wars; and we would find religion transposed into a private extreme and into a mystical suspicion of some controlling malicious Force that connects the Lady V. with all the master cabals of the century.

Mondaugen's story of South West Africa not only demonstrates how humanity is perverted by war and is led to mass annihilation performed with relish, but it includes the perversions of Hedwig Vogelsang whose purpose is to "tantalize and send raving the race of man," and who has sex with Mondaugen only when he is ravaged by scurvy. Veronica the rat is not just the product of Father Fairing's inversion of religious principles; she is also his hope for a postwar society and she is an ambiguous mixture of saint and seducer. Yoyodyne is not simply an unscrupulous producer of weapons; it is another manifestation of V. since it manufactures "Vergeltungswaffe" (destructive reprisal weapons). Anywhere we find the letter V. in Pynchon's book it is connected to sex, war, or conspiracy. History itself, it is suggested, may be nothing more than the "jitterings and squeaks of a metaphysical bedspring."

Each manifestation of V. also shows how the inversion of love and the inversion of religion are controlled by our communal dream of annihilation. Pynchon supplies a definite three-stage pattern for each manifestation: decadence, decline to the inanimate, and then annihilation. The pattern is illustrated by the Lady V. who begins as eighteen-year-old Victoria Wren, believing in her own *virtú*, her power to control the movements of fortune. But later we learn "Victoria was being gradually replaced by V.; something entirely different, for which the young century had as yet no name" (p. 410). As we follow her transformations she becomes progressively more decadent and progressively more inanimate. In the end her hair is false, her feet are artificial, her eye is glass, and in place of a belly button she owns a star sapphire. She has become a Bad Priest, perverting the Word and spirit of religion. More inanimate than animate, she is annihilated by children, taken apart as if she were an object to be dismantled. Thus, the Lady V. is not V. itself but an illustration, a prediction of what V. can be, a symptom of the direction of the twentieth century which is still at the decadent stage but is moving toward the inanimate.

The final image of the book presages an extraordinarily gloomy end to the road of the century and to the mystery of V. Old Stencil is annihilated at sea, quickly, quietly, and totally by accident. While young Stencil pursues his illusion of an "ultimate Plot Which Has No Name," and thinks he is in pursuit of V., we learn that V. does not even provide the paradoxical comfort of a planned conspiracy—our annihilation will have no more meaning than Stencil's accidental death or assassination by the bullet of a random psychotic.

Since Pynchon feels we are still in the decadent stage and have only begun the movement toward the inert and the inanimate, he devotes a good deal of his book to documenting the modes of this century's decadence. " 'A decadence.' " we are told, " 'is a falling-away from what is human, and the further we fall the less human we become. Because we are less human, we foist off the humanity we have lost on inanimate objects and abstract theories' " (p. 405). Decadence makes everyone a sexual object, or a statistic in war, or the object of Conspiracy. Pynchon uses the Whole Sick Crew to illustrate decadence in the stylish set and in modern art—in the users of allusions and painters of cheese danish, in effete sophisticates and "Catatonic Expressionists." The Crew are wastelanders right down to the bar they frequent, where "Time, gentlemen, please" echoes from Eliot's waste land. Aimless and bored, they yo-yo from one stale party to the next. They convert themselves to objects; take the case of Fergus Mixolydian, who, to watch TV, "devised an ingenious sleep-switch, receiving its signal from two electrodes placed on the inner skin of his forearm. When Fergus dropped below a certain level of awareness, the skin resistance increased over a preset value to operate the switch. Fergus thus became an extension of the TV set" (p. 56). Even Rachel Owlglass has her moments of "MG love" when she croons love words to her car and strokes the gear shift. Benny the schlemiel, who cannot live in peace with inanimate objects, becomes himself as inanimate as a yo-yo. Fausto Maijstral has a period when he becomes one with the landscape of the waste land, having "taken on much of the non-humanity of the debris, crushed stone, broken masonry, destroyed churches and auberges of his city" (p. 307).

Pynchon is continually concerned with contemporary indications of the inert and the inanimate and is at least semiserious when he calls the twentieth century a "Neo-Jacobean" age of decadence. His concern is best illustrated by Benny Profane's confrontation with SHROUD (synthetic human, radiation output determined), and SHOCK (synthetic human object, casualty kinematics). SHROUD, a research instrument for Yoyodyne Munitions, measures the effect of radiation fallout, and SHOCK measures the effect of automobile accidents. For Pynchon, they measure two more approaches to twentieth-century annihilation. SHROUD, somehow given the power to make prophetic statements for Benny Profane only, warns him that man is already on his way to nonbeing. Pointing out the similarity between an automobile graveyard and Auschwitz, SHROUD describes for Benny "thousands of Jewish corpses, stacked up like those poor car-bodies. Schlemihl: It's already started" (p. 295). The decadence of the century goes beyond the fitful inanities of the Whole Sick Crew; Pynchon's weaving of fact with fiction, his play upon actual history, and his almanac statistics turn the book from a game with mysteries to a genuine presentation of the mystery of contemporary fact. Locked behind the mystery of V. is not a fantasy for keen readers and would-be secret agents, but the shockingly recognizable facts of our experience.

With the realization that Pynchon means V. to represent a plunge toward annihilation, brought about by our decadence and growing "non-humanity" and based on the facts of twentieth-century inversion of love and religion, we can return to the question that haunts this book and so many others written in the sixties. What Force has gained control over our lives and led us to pursue V., to pursue our own annihilation? Pynchon is very aware that in recent years the fear of conspiracy has become more and more a part of daily news, that "we have men like Stencil, who must go about grouping the world's random caries into cabals" (p. 153). (We might note the present-time action of *V.* begins shortly after the McCarthy Hearings closed.) In lucid moments we may find it hard to believe someone could truly postulate the existence of a real metaphysical force, or a real organization, that with its own logic and malicious purpose is controlling the extremes of modern experience. Without some such logic, however, we may be forced to admit that the intricate fate of our century hangs on nothing purposeful, malicious or otherwise.

By allowing the reader to see more of what goes on than any of the characters do, Pynchon makes it clear that the appearances of V. are not manifestations of a Plot but simple chance events. One of the most effective tensions of the book comes from the reader's desire to make V. into a universal principle of conspiracy even though he has enough contrary information to know that what happened in Florence was a tissue of accidents, that Vheissu is no stronghold for world conspirators, and that old Stencil was not killed by agents of a master cabal who felt he knew too much. We are trapped by the outrageous coincidences of modern fact into wanting to believe that some Force "continues active today and at the moment, because the ultimate Plot Which Has No Name is as yet unrealized." But that desire is exactly what Pynchon means to point out—we seek the logical causes and we construct the fictions that create our problems and result in wars. There is no mysterious force behind V., but there is our misplaced impulse to uncover some Power external to man which is the source of our insane dream of annihilation—the spiritual yearning of wastelanders who live without mythology and feel compelled to construct one from the outrageous but stony materials of modern fact. The period after the V in Pynchon's title leads us to believe there is a word behind the mystery and leads us to turn random symptoms into an unholy kind of Word become flesh. We prove Pynchon's point even as we read: we can accept no God, but we can invent and pursue His inversion. Like all good black humor, Pynchon's comedy about plot and paranoia combines the funny with the horrible and traps our conscience in the combination.

Our own fiction of conspiracies and our own half-wish–
half-fear that some force controls our lives is only one
more symptom of our dream of annihilation. The actual
way in which Conspiracy helps us pursue that dream lies
not in its real existence, but in our paranoid reactions;
we respond to the world as if Conspiracy were true and
our response makes its effect as real as if it did exist—as
real, at least, as the Russo-American arms race.

Plots and conspiracies, then, are illusions. When Pynchon confronts us with the intertwining facts of experience, he wants us to recognize, as Fausto Maijstral
does, that the intertwining is pure accident. We are to
tell ourselves what old Stencil tells himself: "Don't act
as if it were a conscious plot against you. Who knows how
many thousand accidents—a variation in the weather, the
availability of a ship, the failure of a crop—brought all
these people, with their separate dreams and worries,
here to this island and arranged them in this alignment?"
(p. 483). Further, when we look for meanings and purposes in life itself, we must, Pynchon tells us, cease to be
"Tourists" and begin to see beneath the "gaudy skin" to
the heart of human life. Like old Godolphin, standing
alone in the vast waste land at the South Pole, we must
eventually strike through the surface spectacle of things
and discover the essential truth—that there is "Nothing."
This is the discovery of the void, the recognition that we
live in a meaningless waste land with no hope of a Grail
Knight to deliver us, though, still, we live. "There could
have been no more entirely lifeless and empty place anywhere on earth" (p. 205).

But Pynchon does not leave us entirely in so desolate
a place; there are some characters in the book who strike
through to this discovery of the void *and recover,* as if
from the lifeless, to make the same simple affirmation we

have seen to be characteristic of the sixties—"life is the most precious possession you have." Rachel Owlglass, McClintic Sphere, and Fausto Maijstral—each, having faced the waste land and an inanimate rocklike existence, makes some discovery about the nature of love that turns his rock to shelter, just as Eliot's "red rock" becomes a shelter in his waste land. For Fausto the rock is Malta; for redheaded Rachel and for McClintic Sphere, it is the strength they gain from understanding what it means to give, sympathize, and control. Both Rachel and McClintic lose in their attempt to communicate love and both recognize the limitations love has in making life meaningful, but both go on giving and caring. McClintic's recognition is one of the most positive and tender moments of the book: he tells Paola, who is leaving him and whom he loves, that he has not understood things until that moment.

> "Lazy and taking for granted some wonder drug someplace to cure that town, to cure me. Now there isn't and never will be. Nobody is going to step down from heaven and square away Roony and his woman, or Alabama, or South Africa or us and Russia. There's no magic words. Not even I love you is magic enough. Can you see Eisenhower telling Malenkov or Khrushchev that? Ho-ho. Keep cool but care." [p. 366]

Pynchon gives us little else as a counterbalance to our communal dream of annihilation—only the small though decidedly positive communal hope that we can all keep cool but care. And yet, even as McClintic informs Paola of these simple but affirmative sentiments, Pynchon informs us that "somebody had run over a skunk a ways back. The smell had followed them for miles."

Fausto's affirmative stance is undoubtedly meant to be

Pynchon's major alternative to a waste land world running out of alternatives. Although Fausto goes no further than McClintic, giving us nothing more firm than keep cool but care, his regeneration on Malta, "a cradle of life," is decidedly meant to illustrate the possibility of reversing the trend toward annihilation, of coming back from the inanimate and recovering from the scars of war and the sight of V. Having lived through the war and having seen the Lady V. meet her death, Fausto has gained the essential knowledge of life, death, and the twentieth century. He understands V. but has no illusions about conspiracy, for he tells us, "Only one thing matters: it's the bomb that wins" (p. 332). Until his regeneration Fausto's progress from youth to war-weary cynic—from Fausto I to Fausto III—is a model of what Pynchon means by decadence and the movement toward the inanimate. " 'Decadence, decadence,' " Fausto writes, labeling the war-caused split in his personality Fausto II and Fausto III, " 'What is it? Only a clear movement toward death or, preferably, non-humanity. As Fausto II and III, like their island, became more inanimate, they moved closer to the time when like any dead leaf or fragment of metal they'd be finally subject to the laws of physics' " (p. 321).

Fausto hits his lowest point as he inertly watches the children dismantle the Bad Priest, the final avatar of the Lady V. It is then that he becomes "inanimate" and "rocklike," a thing one step from the dead—Fausto III, debris and a ravaged soul, waiting with Malta for his annihilation by bomb. But Fausto recovers; he becomes Fausto IV, who has "inherited a physically and spiritually broken world," a true waste land, and yet somehow finds reason to endure as a living human being. Pynchon never tells us exactly what it is that regenerates Fausto; he himself admits: "Of Fausto III's return to life, little can be said. It happened. What inner resources were there to give it nourishment are still unknown to the present Fausto. This is a confession and in that return from the rock was nothing to confess" (p. 345). Perhaps while kneeling and administering last rites to the dying Lady V., half woman and half inert object, Fausto saw in her the image and the symptom we are all supposed to see. Perhaps with the rubble of a bombed waste land stacked around him he saw the future of the century, the cryptograph V. as a whole, revealing the terror of everyone's annihilation, the terror that all of us could be dismantled by our own future as the children dismantled Lady V. Perhaps Fausto was just not ready to administer last rites to all of human life.

Ultimately, Pynchon wants us to recognize that Malta itself, "the womb of rock," has something to do with Fausto's regeneration. There is much about Pynchon's Malta that could provide an inspiration to survive: it has a mythology, not just the old Knights of Malta, but myths like the history of Mara, teacher of love, told to us by Mehemet the sea captain; it is a place curiously untouched by time, whose people "don't feel the fingers of years jittering age, blindness into face, heart and eyes" (p. 321)—they are not forced into the patterns of history and so perhaps can avoid the decadence that usually accompanies the progress of time. Malta is an island of rock, but instead of being the kind of rock that indicates a waste land of the inanimate, Malta is a rock that sustains its people. Because it is a rock, it is able to withstand the daily bombing it receives in World War II— and because it endures, its people endure. "Malta, and her inhabitants, stood like an immovable rock in the river Fortune, now at war's flood" (p. 325). The Maltese people assign human qualities to their island—"invincibility," "tenacity," "perseverance"—and instead of being themselves led toward decadence, the inanimate, and final annihilation, they emulate their beloved island and learn human endurance from a rock. What Pynchon finds most important is that Fausto and the Maltese people develop a sense of community based on the indestructibility of their rock. Malta teaches them to give, sympathize, and control, or, in McClintic Sphere's more accessible, reduced, war-torn form, to keep cool but care. It is the caring and the giving that makes the Maltese survive and teaches Fausto enough control so that he can return from his vision of annihilation to a simple affirmation of life. Pynchon uses the principle of correspondence mentioned earlier—paralleling the private microcosm with the public or metaphysical macrocosm—to intimate Fausto is reborn because he discovers he can be like Malta and so endure. "As the Ark was to Noah so is the inviolable womb of our Maltese rock to her children" (p. 318).

Nonetheless, to assign any real value to Malta is a "delusion." Pynchon is not suggesting that we see Malta as an ideal place, or even that we see it as a symbol of genuine sanity, like Joseph Heller's use of Sweden at the end of *Catch-22*. Instead, we must admit that it "has no value apart from its function; that it is a device, an artifice" (p. 326). As we have already learned, when you strike beneath the skin of any twentieth-century value, you will find Nothing. Scrutiny of what happened on Malta would show that the communion it supported was as much a result of accident as old Stencil's death was. Any elevation of Malta to a universal principle is an illusion, as V. the conspiracy is an illusion, as a tourist's view of the skin of life is an illusion. What Pynchon has made clear is that in the face of the waste land of this century some kind of illusion is necessary for man to remain human—and that some illusions are better than others. The pursuit of V. is a bad illusion because it leads toward annihilation rather than toward an affirmation of life. By speaking of Malta as a woman and by describing it as a place with a certain absence of color, in contrast to the gaudy colors associated with V., Pynchon makes us compare the illusion of V. with the illusion surrounding Malta. Belief in Malta is a good illusion because it produces a sense of communion and a feeling that man can endure. It is a fruitful illusion, important not because it offers the hope of a new set of absolute values, but because it provides an image of something human in the midst of the inhumanity of war and helps reverse Fausto's movement toward death. Thus, it convinces Fausto of the possibility of his own humanity. "To have humanism," he tells us, "we must first be convinced of our humanity. As we move further into decadence this becomes more difficult" (p. 322).

As we have seen repeatedly in the novel of the sixties, there is only one important quest—to affirm life no matter how negative the facts of experience may be. To do so we may have to create our own illusion, we may have to build our own fable and play the role of the poet, for as Fausto tells us, "It is the 'role' of the poet, this 20th Century. To lie." Our century has gone as far as it can go in destroying old illusions; to regain value one must discover new illusions; the writer, accordingly, may have to become once again the illusion-maker, the fabulist.

Fausto's poet friend makes it clear that lies and illusions are necessary even for the tourists of the world who have never yet recognized the void.

> If I told the truth
> You would not believe me.
> If I said: no fellow soul
> Drops death from the air, no conscious plot
> Drove us underground, you would laugh
> As if I had twitched the wax mouth
> Of my tragic mask into a smile— [p. 326]

Since we must have illusions, Pynchon cautions us, let them be like Malta and not like Herbert Stencil's V.— pick a good dream, not the one about annihilation.

THE POSSIBILITY: A NOTE ON THOMAS PYNCHON'S
The Crying of Lot 49

In *V.* conspiracy is an illusion, but in *The Crying of Lot 49* Pynchon seriously considers the possibility that conspiracies could exist. The range of this much shorter and less impressive second novel has been narrowed; Pynchon's imagination is as fertile as ever, but he is almost entirely concerned with a single question: what possibilities are left for twentieth-century man, particularly in America? The novel is built around the pursuit of Tristero, a mystery manifested in an underground organization dating from about 1300 which has challenged the established postal systems of the world and has concentrated on America since about 1853. Tristero has represented the disinherited, has operated for the use of the alienated, and has been a constant threat of ominous destruction. Although Tristero is as omnipresent as V., the pursuit of this desperate mystery is not like the pursuit of V. In one sense, V. is a metaphor for the direction in which the contemporary world is headed, but Tristero is a metaphor for the narrow scope of contemporary human possibilities or alternatives. Therefore, we may trace our alternatives in an examination of the Tristero Conspiracy: either Tristero exists or it does not exist. If it exists, it is either malevolent or benevolent; it is the instrument of our annihilation or it provides a whole new means of human communication, an escape from human isolation and from the arid inanities of contemporary life. If it does not exist, then we are all trapped in an "orbiting" paranoia that could provide the solace of a new fantasy, a new illusion, or could initiate a spiral ending in madness. Our only remaining possibility is that Tristero is a put-on; Pynchon, the black humorist, could be putting us on, or Oedipa Maas, the heroine who pursues the mystery of Tristero, could be a victim of a joke.

Oedipa begins the book as an unaware housewife coming home from a tupperware party slightly tipsy because there was too much kirsch in the fondue, and she slowly grows to become a kind of Everyman. But in Pynchon's world, all human possibilities (represented by Tristero) seem to be created for man and imposed on him from some mysterious and external force; the individual, the Everyman, has no control over those possibilities. Consequently, like all of us, the heroine of the novel is helpless, and she remains helpless even as she becomes a kind of "activist." She is a searcher, but more like a passive reader of mysteries—a scholar and pursuer of footnotes—than like an active source of new possibilities. In pursuing Tristero Oedipa discovers the absence of any Grail Knight, for, as we are told, she is trapped as if in a tower by "magic, anonymous and malignant, visited on her from outside and for no reason at all;" and she slowly discovers that "the tower is everywhere and the knight of deliverance [is] no proof against its magic." [4] Tristero compels her to seek her own deliverance; it leads her to understand the range of her alternatives, but neither she nor we ever learn which possibilities are truths and which are lies, for the ultimate possibility of the book, the ultimate answer to every man's deliverance, and the ultimate meaning of Tristero are never revealed.

In the last image of the book—the image of Oedipa locked in a room surrounded by black-suited men who are probably the agents of Tristero, and who will probably reveal to Oedipa that she and we are to be annihilated, or that we are paranoid, or that new "vistas of space and time" await us—in this last image, I believe, Pynchon characterizes the dominant mood of both the American novel and the American culture in the sixties, particularly in the second half of the decade. Made passive by the fear of external forces, we are simply waiting—picketing and protesting, perhaps, but waiting in any case—waiting for a new revelation, for new alternatives. Waiting as if we were in some great planned transitional stage. Waiting as Oedipa does and as John Barth does in *Giles Goat-Boy* for civilization to evolve beyond the oedipal stage, beyond the jealous struggle for power between man and unseen, unknown father-forces. Waiting with George and Martha at the end of *Who's Afraid of Virginia Woolf?* for another round of exorcism, another onslaught from some unknown big bad wolf. The primary value, thematically, of Pynchon's flawed but tightly coiled second novel lies in the precision with which he summarizes our alternatives and our state of mind in the

4. *The Crying of Lot 49*, pp. 21–22. Page numbers for all further citations will be included parenthetically in the text.

sixties. We await a new revelation—the idea even runs through the social criticism of the sixties, from Richard Poirier and Benjamin DeMott through Theodore Roszak and Charles Reich. In Poirier's controversial article, "The War Against the Young," he tells us that "seldom in the history of modern civilization has there been a greater need felt by everyone for a new key to our mythologies, a key that we nervously feel is about to be found." [5] Either we are waiting for our death or we await an alternative—perhaps a new mythology—to move us beyond the waste land. That is what Oedipa does as she awaits the revelation of the Tristero Conspiracy, whose motto is W.A.S.T.E.—We Await Silent Tristero's Empire.

The word *revelation* is used throughout *The Crying of Lot 49*. Oedipa, alone in her car at the beginning of her search, feels the sense of some concealed meaning. "A revelation also trembled just past the threshold of her understanding . . . she seemed parked at the centre of an odd, religious instant. As if, on some other frequency, or out of the eye of some whirlwind rotating too slow for her heated skin even to feel the centrifugal coolness of, words were being spoken" (pp. 24–25). It is as if Job's God were soon to speak from the whirlwind revealing an unheard sacred mystery. This feeling lingers throughout the book, sometimes striking us with terror for what the revelation will be, at other times making us wonder if Pynchon is not really reaching behind contemporary fact to find some hope that a new mystery quivering to be heard could also be a saving mystery. Revelation could, then, be a metaphor for the life and death *urgency in time* of our discovering a new set of alternatives, or a metaphoric plea that we develop a liberating use of the imagination (as the social critics also plead), or it could

5. *The Atlantic Monthly,* Oct. 1968, p. 61.

literally be the appearance of some actual savior who will settle our world in a single stroke. It is the measure of Pynchon's fear that time is running out and man's awareness is woefully lacking. But he also feels that something is emerging. The question for Pynchon and for other novelists in the sixties is what will emerge first; what will be revealed to us: annihilation or alternatives.

And so, Oedipa ends by waiting:

> The waiting above all; if not for another set of possibilities to replace those that had conditioned the land . . . then at least, at the very least, waiting for a symmetry of choices to break down, to go skew. . . . For it is now like walking among the matrices of a great digital computer, the zeroes and ones twined above. . . . Another mode of meaning behind the obvious, or none; either a transcendent meaning, or only the earth. [p. 181]

Human alternatives break down into believing everything or nothing, one or zero—believing in flag, country, computer, bomb, and benevolent deity, or believing in chaos, annihilation, and man as atoms in motion. Nonetheless, whether Tristero exists or not, Oedipa *does* close the novel by sitting in that frightening room; the door *is* locked, and those men in black *do* seem to threaten. Not only is the threat of a malicious conspiracy kept alive in those final moments, but even at best, even if we are waiting for Tristero to be the revelation of a new alternative, a new mode of communication, we are undoubtedly beset by terror as we wait. The pursuit of possibility in the sixties is vitiated by the fear that we may really find something which has control over our lives. Both Oedipa Maas and Ralph Ellison's narrator in *Invisible Man* step outside history to discover the pos-

sibilities of the underground world. Oedipa discovers
W.A.S.T.E., and the invisible man discovers the super-
hip world of Rinehart. Ellison's narrator, operating in
the world of the fifties, is led to discover that there is
"an element of criminality in freedom," and in criminality and freedom lies a world of possibility, a reason to
celebrate. Pynchon's Oedipa learns that possibility could
also mean the horror of conspiracy, and conspiracy is
darkly intertwined with the revelation of any new alternative. In that alternative, in that revelation, and in that
possibility lies the unshakable persistence of terror.

6: CONSPIRACY FROM WITHOUT AND WITHIN

TERROR, GUILT, AND DESIRE: THE UNCONSCIOUS
AS CONSPIRATOR

While Thomas Pynchon shows us the terror of our communal and public dream of death, John Hawkes explores the individual's dream, and the violent terror—the lust for death—that haunts the heart of that dream. The individual in *The Lime Twig*, Michael Banks, is literally run over by a power evoked from his own unconscious desires in conspiracy with a malevolent external force. The symbolic racehorse, set in motion by Michael's submerged desires and managed by a gang of metaphysical thugs, destroys Michael, running him down at the racetrack where Michael and the gang set it running. It is an instructive image, capturing the full meaning of the power that has usurped control over the individual's life, at least according to Hawkes. The mad dream of death that seems a force imposed upon us from the outside—someone else's bomb, or someone else's racehorse—really begins with our own individual unconscious desires. When those desires join forces with the conditions of a waste land world, they form a dreamlike conspiracy that sets in motion the dream annihilation both Hawkes and Pynchon fear. Hawkes's characters, as we shall see, are wastelanders trapped and longing for release through death. The terror of *The Lime Twig* lies, in part, in our discovery that this longing is the cohort of all the forces we fear.

At times, the drama, the film, and the novel of the sixties have attempted to create some powerful single image, like Hawkes's racetrack death, that can catch the contemporary sense of terror. We recall, again, the image of George and Martha at the end of Albee's *Who's Afraid of Virginia Woolf?* They are huddled together, filled with terror over a nameless power they call Virginia Woolf, a mystery whose source is surely in their own individual unconscious desires and guilts. Or there is Antonioni's film, *Blow-up* (an ominous title), with its image of a sylvan love scene—man and woman, hand in hand, romping over romantically green grass—until the scene is blown-up and blown-up, and we discover a lurking terror: a hand with a gun, the possibility of a plot, where love has led the man in the picture not to pastoral delights but to death. It is a good idea to think in terms of images when talking about *The Lime Twig* because Hawkes uses them much as they are used in film, attempting to inform us of several things simultaneously; for example, Hawkes conveys the theme of victims and victimization through the background recurrence of bird and children images.

Before going on with a discussion of *The Lime Twig*, it might be useful to point out for contrast two novels which employ a simplified pattern of externalizing unconscious guilts and fears into some terrifying force, conspiracy, or shadow that threatens doom. *DeFord* by David

Shetzline and *Listen Ruben Fontanez* by Jay Neugeboren are both about old men with failing hearts who are haunted by certain shadows: Shetzline's hero is pursued by a drunken Indian, Joe Raven; and Neugeboren's hero is threatened by a black teenager seeking revenge for his brother. While the pursuers are both decidedly real and menacing, they are also objectifications of the pursued old men's guilts; the point is clear enough to delight Leslie Fiedler, if he knows of these two books. The atmosphere of both novels is the threatening tensions of contemporary urban life—life in the "Unreal City," as Eliot calls it.

Listen Ruben Fontanez is by far the better book. It is a warm and modest novel that seems unbothered by the usual impulse to construct themes. The hero, pursued by his guilts and the young Black, learns to be more human and saves himself with the help of a young Puerto Rican. *DeFord,* although somewhat clumsy, can serve as a pattern for how a great many current novels deal with guilt, desire, and terror. The guilt or desire shows itself first as a product of the unconscious, as a dream.

> An old man named DeFord lay dying, mind slipping away, body already numbed as he dreamed of an Indian hauling twisted legs up his stairs, left hand clutching an ice pick. On his back DeFord heard and saw the crippled Indian—now on the stairs, now at the door, now in his room—the ice pick raised, dark face pinched with hate. He struggled in his dream's envelope while his heart only quivered, its habit forgotten.[1]

The dream next becomes a real presence that seeks the dreamer's death, and the real presence in turn becomes

1. *DeFord,* p. 4.

a universal principle—a conspiracy, a devil, or, as in this case, just an abstract threat. "The presence of Raven was terror, as shapeless as the dark of one's childhood, void of form or habit, without reason, mind or language. It was bottomless horror—the same abyss that threatened when you stopped whatever you were doing and asked questions. It was what lay beneath when you plunged. Faceless, twisted, mindless" (p. 116). In the end, the old man learns the quality of his guilt and just as if the unconscious withdrew its secret menacing because it had been discovered, Joe Raven shrinks to human size and loses his prey. The old man confesses "remorse and guilt were less oppressive than fear." There is, of course, no complete victory, but DeFord has grappled with the specter from his own unconscious mind and beaten it by learning to recognize and cope with his guilt. To further identify our ignorance of man's unconscious tensions, Shetzline adds a kind of subplot in which an ex-businessman blames his specters on Conspiracy. Dee Bee Smith, derelict and fugitive from "Them," is an example of the man who never recognizes that what terrorizes him has its origin in himself. Still, he too escapes the Conspirators that haunt him, and Shetzline leaves us with some small mystery of doubt whether there might not be some external force that conspires against us—even if we are pretty sure it is our own unconscious fears, desires, and guilts.

The Lime Twig's exploration of man's unconscious lust for death is a much more profound and complex version of Shetzline's pattern. For one thing, Michael Banks does not get off as easily as DeFord does once he has set loose his unconscious forces to conspire with the external world. Hawkes is far more convincing because he realizes you cannot call back the wheel of fire once you have set it rolling—and certainly you cannot call it back by the simple recognition that you are the one who launched it. *The Lime Twig* encompasses many of the themes and methods characteristic of the novel of the sixties: the use of the waste land image, for example, the blurring of fact and fiction, and the exploration of forces that rule our lives. Hawkes closely parallels Joseph Heller and Jerome Charyn in his concentration on the cycle of victims and victimizers, using children to symbolize the brutality of inherited habit. Like Pynchon, Hawkes finds love to be limited in value, and the perversion of love to be at the core of man's mad passion for death. As Hencher pursues his love and Michael pursues his desires, we find they both really pursue their destruction; the exposure of the unconscious is for Hawkes something like the unveiling of Pynchon's V. Love in the waste land is always perverted because of fear, twisting itself into a hidden desire for the temptress, for the belladonna, which in Michael Banks's case means lust for Sybilline, or, as we shall see, lust for death.

But the internal unconscious desires that launch Banks on his pursuit of destruction are not the whole cause of that destruction; there are external conditions that conspire with Michael's desires, and the two together do him in. There is something decidedly demonic about the world and Hawkes attempts to convey external evil through Larry and his gang. But the images are purposely ambiguous, and Larry comes out at times an angel, at times a devil. He could be entirely the symbolic fulfiller of Michael's dream-wishes, or he could be a very real mobster who has planned the whole crime, setting Hencher onto Michael to get the plot rolling by convincing Michael to steal the ancient horse Rock Castle and enter him in the "Golden Bowl" at Aldington. One of the key mysteries in Hawkes's vision is how much control the unconscious has over man's life and how much control external forces have. Hawkes himself speaks, in an interview, of his "belief in the terrifying existence of Satanism in the world." [2] So, we wonder—is there really some external satanic force, a gang, conspirators? or by Satanism does Hawkes mean the piled-up evils that result from the complex intertwining of many men acting out their unconscious desires, fears, and guilts? In the end, Hawkes finds the single individual's unconscious mind to be the primary force that leads to evil. Thus, we return to the image of the racehorse set in motion; it is Banks who sets the race going and it is only Banks who can stop it. But the conspiracy between man's unconscious desires and the brutal facts of the external world terrorizes the individual, makes his life a dream of death, so that to stop the race and end the rule of this conspiracy costs Banks his life.

Like Eliot's *Waste Land*, *The Lime Twig* is constructed from the mixture of memory and desire. The prologue of the book is Hencher's memory of his youth, of the war, and of his mother love. Hencher, by pursuing an equivalent to his lost mother love, begins to love both Michael and Margaret Banks. His love is obsessive, and finds outlet first in a well-prepared breakfast in bed for the married couple, and then in the introduction of a plan that sets in motion all of Michael's submerged desires and some of Margaret's. The ultimate result is the perversion of love during one orgiastic night when Michael takes on almost as many women as wishes make, and Margaret is punished for his deviation—but punished in a way connected to her own wishes. Hencher, conse-

2. "John Hawkes on His Novels," *Massachusetts Review* 7 (Summer 1966): 449–61.

quently, is the henchman who links the memory section
of the book to the desire section, the prologue to the
body of the book. Although there seems to be a past time
and a present time, Hawkes, like Eliot, works to show the
ever-present contemporaneity of the past. There are a
great many mysterious correspondences between Hencher's memories and the actions in the present time of
the book. For example, Hencher remembers a small
man named Sparrow who was hooked on morphine and
begrudged the drug's being given to Hencher's mother.
There is also a small man named Sparrow in Larry's
gang who operates in the present. He too needs morphine.
Many of the other correspondences are verbal echoes—
children, birds, pearls, dogs. The looming sense of death
that Hencher describes during the war—fear of fire starting everywhere, fear of explosion, fear of the crash land-
ing of a disabled British plane—this sense of death also
hangs over the present time of the book, evoked by the
violent quality of Michael's desires.

Rock Castle, the horse that symbolizes desire itself, is
timeless, a thing of cyclical reappearance. Because memory, desire, and the threat of death are outside of time,
Hawkes destroys the categories of time, and all actions
are significant only as they define the waste land created
by terror and desire. Like Eliot's neurasthenic woman,
Hawkes's Sybilline is defined not by her single appearance
in time, but by a collection of timeless images making her
the Cleopatra of infinite variety, the modern Madame
Sosostris, a false prophet, the eternal Sibyl, and all other
timeless belladonnas. Not only are memory and desire
timeless, but their effect on man's life has been ageless.
So, Hencher's memory-love snares him as Michael's desires do, and love repressed or love misdirected becomes
a lust for death—the mixing of memory and desire sym-

bolizes the timeless snare that captures its victims like birds on a lime twig. As the barge carrying Michael's dream horse docks in the fog, we are told of the timelessness of the waste land. "It was not Wednesday at all, only a time slipped off its cycle with hours and darkness never to be accounted for." [3] With time slipped off its cycle the action of the book moves as in a dream, forcing its images upon the reader as if he were locked in an eternal waste land April, trapping him in a cruel mixture of memory and desire where the search for love leads to terror and he is "shown fear in a handful of dust."

Although the idea for stealing the horse, Rock Castle, is proposed by Hencher, who is a member of the gang led by Larry, and all the procuring and arranging to get the horse into the Golden Bowl race at Aldington is done by Larry, the whole process—the major action of the novel—exists only because Michael dreams and wishes it into existence. Larry and his gang are the brute facts of experience, but they are given their power, as if evoked, through Michael's dream. Michael is a safe middle-class property owner, but an aimless, bored wastelander. "So we lead our lives," Hencher says of he and Michael and Margaret, "keep our privacy in Dreary Station, spend our days grubbing at the rubber roots, pausing at each other's doors" (p. 27). Michael lives, indeed, in a dreary station and the grubbing at rubber roots echoes Eliot's question, "What are the roots that clutch, what branches grow / Out of this stony rubbish?"

All Michael seems to have in his pallid life are his unconscious wishes and desires, and the only branch they grow is the ensnaring lime twig. His secret dreams cause the action of the novel and this is the only kind of cause

3. *The Lime Twig*, p. 50. Page numbers for all further citations will be included parenthetically in the text.

and effect relationship in Hawkes's world. Even when the acting out of Michael's desires becomes intertwined with Margaret's dream, they still remain the root and cause of all the suffering. Here is the first conjuration of Michael's dream, a vision of the horse he desires:

> His own worst dream, and best, was of a horse which was itself the flesh of all violent dreams; knowing this dream, that the horse was in their sitting room—he had left the flat door open as if he meant to return in a moment or meant never to return—seeing the room empty except for moonlight bright as day and, in the middle of the floor, the tall upright shape of the horse draped from head to tail in an enormous sheet that falls over the eyes and hangs down stiffly from the silver jaw; knowing the horse on sight and listening while it raises one shadowed hoof on the end of a silver thread of foreleg and drives down the hoof to splinter in a single crash one plank of that empty Dreary Station floor. [p. 33]

This is really a vision, but the vision and the wish become flesh when Michael actually does get the horse— Rock Castle—and the vision becomes prophecy as the horse becomes the flesh of all violent dreams, shattering Michael's life and home like the shattered plank envisioned at Dreary Station. The horse is Michael's own worst dream, and best—it is his worst dream because of the violence and death it leads to, and it is his best dream because, curiously enough, it leads to his redemption. To understand the dream, let us look at what it sets in motion: Larry, Sybilline, and Rock Castle are the three major specters conjured up by Michael's dreams. They are also living creatures who represent certain brute facts about the external world. Understanding them will help us understand the conspiracy that leads to Michael's death.

Larry, leader of the mob, is a mysterious specter who is variously described as an angel full of grace, as a devil full of murder, as a fish full of destructive lust, and as a human being who is a petty mobster hoping to make his bundle and retire. People shine his shoes for him, take off their hats when they talk to him, and obey him as if he were God's law. When we first see him he is described as being "heavy as a horse" (linking him to Rock Castle), but solid, dangerous, impersonal—"an impassive escort who, by chance, could touch a woman's breast in public easily, with propriety, offending no one" (p. 74). There is something machinelike about him. He is never without his vest of linked steel and his shoulder-worn pistol. His actions seem necessary, as if he by himself were the principle of external law—the law, that is, that inflicts punishment. When he cuts Margaret and rapes her—after she has been beaten by his henchman, Thick—Larry seems to be moving by necessity, as if he were compelled by Margaret's dream and Michael's immoral orgy at the Widow's house. (The scene of Margaret's torment comes before Michael's orgy in the book, but Hawkes makes it clear that the orgy began at 2 A.M. and the torment afterward at 4 A.M.) As a fulfiller of wishes he is Larry the fairy godfather, "Larry who was an angel if any angel ever had eyes like his or flesh like his" (p. 83). If we see him as an angel, then he must be the angel of deliverance, helping satisfy the hidden desires of others, or the angel of retribution, punishing swiftly what are undoubtedly the immoral lusts of Michael and even Margaret. In what other way could he be "full-of-grace"?

Larry also hints at the demonic—murderer of Cowles the trainer and surely a great many others, exploiter of

Michael's hidden dreams, jailer and torturer, he is the moving force behind a great deal of "deviltry." The linked steel vest, the "brass knuckles shining on enormous hands," the eyes "devoid of irises," the "hairless and swarthy torso of the man himself" make us feel there is something inhuman about him. When Sydney Slyter, the sportswriter whose column prefaces every chapter in *The Lime Twig*, says that somebody—"angel of Heaven or Hell"—must have known what they were doing when they stole Rock Castle and entered him in the Golden Bowl race, he can only mean Larry, for the only other force behind the act was Michael's unconscious desire. So Larry is a force, both angelic and demonic—or perhaps neither. When he descends upon the beaten and cut Margaret, she sees his body dressed only in the bulletproof vest, and notes "the shining links like fish scales." Larry is the fish brought to the surface by Michael and Margaret's desires, but instead of the simple fertility symbol sought by the wounded Fisher King, they have landed an inverted symbol of potential self-violence and death. If Larry exists to terrorize and destroy, it is because the everyday dreamer, the middle-class average Michael, can fish him up from his own submerged being and set him on his way.

But on the other hand, Larry is really a racetrack thug who has planned a cute deal where he can win a lot of money on a stolen horse that is a sure thing, and he cannot get caught because he has used a straight citizen for his patsy. He, too, is a man with dreams, telling his lady cohort: "I'll make it up to you. I'll make it up for the twenty years. A bit of marriage, eh? And then a ship, trees with limes on the branches, niggers to pull us around the streets, the Americas—a proper cruise, plenty of time at the bar, no gunplay or nags. Perhaps a child or two, who knows" (p. 165). On one level, he too is a man driven by his own unconscious demands, a victim as well as a victimizer. But this particular wish rings with irony—especially the "limes on the branches"—and taken all together Larry is neither the complete creation of Michael's unconscious nor a simple everyday crook. He is the ambiguous mystery of external fact; he partakes of all the identities we have seen because, like the actual mystery of fact in the waste land, he is capable of anything, ready to respond to any human desire, fear, or guilt, whether it is good or bad. As Hawkes sees it, the external world is a place of chance occurrence, but the facts of experience are so varied and mysterious that there is always some circumstance to respond to a dreamer's wish. There is always some Larry who will conspire with man's unconscious being and help him pursue fulfillment. This, again, is where the terror lies, for among all the possible dreams that could be pursued through the conspiracy of man's unconscious with the external facts of existence, the one we seem to pursue is the dream of death. Such a dream, for Hawkes and Pynchon both, is the final inversion of the modern waste land. It is in this sense only that Michael's unconscious desire gains control over his life and over him.

Sybilline is also a mysterious mixture of conjured-up specter and real, redheaded, gangland moll. She is the fulfillment of Michael's sexual fantasies, but she is a perverter of love, a "Belladonna, the Lady of the Rocks, / The lady of situations," as Eliot would call her. When Michael first meets Sybilline he thinks he hears in her voice "laughter, motor cars and lovely moonlit trees, beds and silk stockings in the middle of the floor" (p. 120). And that is precisely, detail for detail, what she turns out to be. As with Rock Castle, Michael's vision

of Sybilline comes to be a prophecy and her definition.
This is a clear indication that she too is essentially an
evocation from Michael's subconscious. As such, she provides quite a romp for Michael, who dreams himself a
dream worthy of a sexual Cecil B. DeMille. In one night
Michael frolics with Sybilline, performing exquisitely
three times, and tumbles once with the plump Widow,
once with Annie (a neighbor conjured up on the spot
while Michael is in a winning way), and once even with
frumpy, misanthropic Little Dora. If by this point in
the novel we do not already realize we are seeing the
acting out of a man's secret desires, Michael's champion-
ship studding should certainly tip the case. Michael fan-
cies himself enamored of Sybilline and his guilt over
betraying Margaret is very short-lived. But it is not love
that Michael is pursuing; it is the waste land perversion
of love. The clue is in Sybilline's name; she is the Sibyl
in the epigraph to *The Waste Land,* eternal but eternally
symbolizing the longing for death. This is the buried key
to Michael's unconscious desire—to want Sybilline is to
make the Sibyl's wish, the wish to die, and that wish
determines Michael's dream and the action of the book.
It is this Sibyl, the image of the shrunken specter that
haunts the waste land and the unconscious being, which
is Hawkes's buried source of terror.

In a personal interview Hawkes tells us that Michael
"is moving toward the fulfillment of dreams we ordi-
narily think of as illicit or illegal dreams of a destructive
love." [4] Sybilline is part of that fulfillment, but Margaret's punishment is another part. Larry goes from the
party where Michael has had his romp directly to the
room where Margaret is kept, and like an angel of retribution with some strange sense of justice, he punishes

4. "John Hawkes on His Novels," p. 454.

Margaret for Michael's dream. Margaret, of course, has had her own dreams which are partially responsible.

> She would dream of the crostics and, in the dark, men with numbers wrapped around their fingers would feel her legs, or she would lie with an obscure member of the government on a leather couch, trying to remember and all the while begging for his name. [p. 68]

> She was Banks' wife by the law, she was Margaret, and if the men ever did get hold of her and go at her with their truncheons or knives or knuckles, she would still be merely Margaret. [p. 70]

Her dreams, like Michael's, anticipate their fulfillment, and the long truncheon beating she gets from Thick (with all its overt sexuality) is the clearest indication in the book that our unconscious desires harbor the very actions that terrorize us. It would be a simple step to objectify those desires and call the result a Conspiracy. Hawkes, like Pynchon and Eliot, finds a certain deep immorality coloring man's response to love; but Hawkes, more than the others, shows that love can not only be inadequate as a means for affirmation, it can lead to an unwilling embrace of violence and terror. Perhaps this is what makes Hawkes seem more negative than he is— for while his book ends with an affirmation, he insists that the insanity, immorality, and longing for death that characterizes the contemporary waste land and terrorizes us begins with neither an institution nor an external conspiracy, but with the dark workings of our own soul in need of love. The revelation is not new, but the discovery that we wish for our own truncheon, our own death, or, on Pynchon's level, our own worldwide annihilation, is still startling—startling and politically upsetting when we realize how many public Michaels there are who have the large-scale means so close at hand to make us their beaten Margarets, if we do not do it ourselves.

The horse that Michael produces through Larry and the gang represents the very nature of desire itself. Rock Castle is as ancient as desire; he is "the flesh of all violent dreams"; he has "the fluted and tapering neck of some serpent," suggesting the eternal evil. Handling him is compared by Hencher to lifting bombs out of craters. In short, desire is eternal and eternally menacing. We learn more about Rock Castle from Sydney Slyter, who, although an impotent prophet, at least recognizes the threat the horse poses. He tells us Rock Castle is "rigid, fixed; a prison of heritage in the victorious form; the gray shape that forever rages out round the ring of painted horses with the band music piping and clacking; indomitable" (p. 124). The image is clear—desire is fixed and rigid and always victorious; it is a determining force and a necessary heritage, making of us creatures as unfree as the wooden horses in a merry-go-round. Slyter also tells us that "the fact of this Rock Castle—torn from his mare—predetermined the stallion's cyclic emergence again and again" (p. 139). Desire is a fact which will appear repeatedly; whether evoked by Michael or someone else, its existence is eternal and the thrust of its appearance is assured, at least from time to time. Desire, then, can be a prison of heritage—it can mean man's life is entirely determined. But Hawkes has Michael stop Rock Castle at the very end, and so man does have some control over his own life.

Taken together then, Larry, Sybilline, and Rock Castle explain the basic nature of the conspiracy between the inner world of Michael's unconscious being and the

outer world of brutal, random fact; and they illustrate
how that conspiracy has gained control over Michael's
life. On one level, Larry is the eternal mystery of fact;
Sybilline is the eternal Sibyl, making a death wish out of
love; and Rock Castle is the eternal power of desire.
Together they seem to predetermine man's defeat; they
form the widest kind of prison of heritage. Hawkes's
waste land of memory and desire is timeless because the
forces that control it are eternal and pass from one generation to the next. The vision is similar to the world
of victims and victimizers we saw in Joseph Heller's
Catch-22. As Heller puts it, "Every victim was a culprit,
every culprit a victim, and somebody had to stand up
sometime to try and break the lousy chain of inherited
habit that was imperiling them all." [5] The difference for
Hawkes is that the chain is made mostly from internal
and unconscious links; thus, the cost of trying to break
that chain is far greater for Michael Banks than it is for
Heller's Yossarian. Before we look at Michael's success,
let us look first at Hawkes's vision of a determined world
—his prison of heritage, the parade of victims and victimizers.

Michael and Margaret are identified with a series of
suffering-child images that appear throughout the novel.
The images are initiated by Hencher's picture of a little
boy in an alley "slick with gray goose slime," who every
day performs a ritual of loving scrutiny over his dog.
But what we remember about the boy are the unex-
plained details: "The whipping marks were always fresh
on his legs and one cheekbone was blue" (p. 8). From
this point on, suffering children form a wailing background for almost every significant act taken by Margaret
or Michael which traps them deeper in their desires:

5. *Catch-22*, p. 414.

children fill the air with noise as Michael begins his
venture on the ironically named *Artemis*; when Michael
calls Margaret and summons her to come to the track,
his voice on the telephone is mingled with a "click and
a child wailing somewhere down the row"; as Margaret
proceeds by train to meet Michael and is approached by
the first member of Larry's mob, she has a vision which
begins when she "felt the wobbling tracks running over
the ties, and each tie crushed under the wheels became a
child. Children were tied down the length of track: she
saw the toads hopping off their bodies at the first whisper
of wheels, the faint rattling of oncoming rods and chains,
and she saw the sparks hitting the pale heads and feet"
(pp. 70–71).

The background images of children can serve as
prophecies of the approaching victimization of Margaret
or Michael. When Margaret is led off to the room where
her beating will take place she hears "the sounds of an
infant crying and sucking too." The most important
image of a suffering child is represented by the girl
Monica—unwanted daughter of Sybilline—who joins her
moans to Margaret's; who has her own child's nightmares which become indistinguishable from Margaret's;
and who, finally, is the mysterious child in the green
dress, inexplicably murdered by a constable—a cruelty
that inspires Michael's redemptive actions. Monica completes the connection of Margaret and Michael with vic-
timized children. After Margaret has been beaten, her
identification with Monica is complete, and we are told:
she "was a child anything could be done to—and now,
now a docile captive. And when Monica, the little girl,
awoke about this hour with her nightmares, Margaret
took them to be her own bad dreams, as if in soothing
the child she could soothe herself" (p. 126).

When Margaret and Monica set up their joint wail, the image is a sufferer's nightmare. Hawkes uses children to catch an image of the terror in the suffering inflicted on man from generation to generation—the terror of control by an inheritance passed on eternally. We suffer as helplessly as children do, and when we cease to be sufferers, our desires turn us into inflicters of pain, victimizers. This is what Hawkes means by a determining "prison of heritage." So, the detectives at the end of the book will beat their children that night because they have had a bad rainy day, and Larry inflicts punishment on Margaret and Michael as if they were erring children. The process is explained by Little Dora, Margaret's grotesque keeper—she tells how she was shuffled aside as a child, "parked out" more than she was at home; but now she is on the giving end, now things are different. " 'Well,' " she reflects as she reaches an icy hand toward Margaret, " 'it used to be parking out for me. . . . But that's past. Now it's my sister leaves her kids with me of a weekend or summer. And I'm at the good end, now' " (pp. 71–72). To be at the good end means to be the victimizer, for Little Dora watches over Monica, whose suffering and death make her one of the critical victims of the novel.

Before we look at how Monica and the image of the suffering child relates to Michael's redemption, let us examine another set of images which make even clearer that Hawkes's people are trapped and suffering victims. The title of the book intimates that the world of the novel is a lime twig—lime twigs are usually snares for birds. The snare, of course, is the conspiracy of desire with external random facts, but Hawkes makes our pathetic helplessness even more clear when he identifies Michael and Margaret with bird images. As with the different images of suffering children, birds appear at every juncture where Michael or Margaret takes some new step toward destruction. The images become prophecies of some new terror waiting to occur: just before Hencher brings Michael and Margaret their breakfast in bed—the breakfast initiating a dance of love that becomes a dance of death—we learn, "one of the gulls came round from the kitchen and started beating the glass"; just before Michael discovers the death of Hencher he hears "the sound, compact, malcontent, of a hive of bees stinging to death a sparrow"; when Margaret is beaten the truncheon "made a sound like a dead bird falling to empty field." The point is made most clearly at the end of Margaret's beating when she hears a bird, an oven tit, stirring outside the window, "fluttering now and then or scratching, making no attempt to disguise the mood, the pallidness, which later it would affect to conceal in liveliness and muted song. A warbler. But a sleepless bird and irritable" (p. 135). The bird begins its song as Larry commits the last torment on Margaret's beaten body. The mate of the oven tit shows up at the end of Michael's wild sexual party: "The mate of the oven tit had found a branch outside his window and he heard its damp scratching and its talk. Even two oven tits may be snared and separated in such a dawn" (p. 159). The image appearing in both scenes helps make the connection between Michael's indulgent and sinful night and Margaret's painful punishment; it also makes clear that Michael and Margaret are snared victims. They have been caught on the lime twig of desire and Hawkes seeks our compassion for the victim more than our condemnation of the death-dreamer and victimizer. The overall effect of using both the image of the suffering child and the image of the victim bird is extremely subtle, for ultimately these images lead us to an undefined sense of terror whenever birds or children appear, since we know their appearance presages new horrors for Michael and Margaret. It is a brilliant tension created by Hawkes to intensify the atmosphere of nightmare in his book—after all, it can only be a nightmare world when the image of a bird or a child evokes terror.

The idea of a world where children suffer simply because they inherit desire and because they are at the mercy of other people's desire—the idea of a world where man is as frail and helpless in the presence of his own desires conspiring with a waste land of random fact as a bird in the presence of a lime twig—this kind of idea obviously indicates a closed and determined world. There is no doubt that Hawkes sees man as an eternal victim in a waste land of memory and desire, but Hawkes is involved with the *individual's* dream, and all the evil that evolves from Michael's unconscious desires can also be controlled by Michael. (In many ways Hawkes, like Pynchon, calls upon very traditional morality: for example, Rock Castle, with its connections to the serpent, is the evil of man's desires, and redemption lies in the control of those desires.) Man, at least in this way, can have some control over his own life; though it costs his death, Michael stops the race. Man is and will be a victim, but he can also be redeemed. The complex idea of a redeemed victim is again conveyed, to a large extent, through Hawkes's imagery. First Michael moves to help the little girl Monica, killed brutally by a constable— the shot rings out after Michael's orgy and he sees the oven tit, the warbler that symbolizes his trap, "flying straight up from the thick brown tree with its song turned into a high and piping whistle." Michael runs to help with "his arms flung wide," in a crucifixion pose. The

incident gives him some insight into the nature of brutal
victimization; he becomes one with the bird, the child,
and the crucified man. Almost exactly the same configuration of images occurs at the racetrack where Michael
"knew he must put a stop to it." Here we learn he has
the heart of a suffering child, for as he ran to stop Rock
Castle "the child pounded on his heart"; and he has
the soul of the snared victim bird, for just as he approaches the thundering horses he gasps for breath and
sees "a dove bursting with air on a bough." But he also
has the power of a man who wishes to be redeemed, and
so he sacrifices himself beneath the fallen horses, striking
again the crucifixion pose, "the arms are out, the head
thrown back."

The suffering child, the victim dove, the redeeming
crucifixion pose, and the symbol of fallen destructive
desire create a combined image more complex than any
of those examples mentioned at the beginning of this
chapter—an image that catches man in his total relationship to the forces that rule his world. On the negative side, Michael has fulfilled his longing for death; the
Golden Bowl is ironically consummated; as Sydney
Slyter puts it, "There is no pathetic fun or mournful
frolic like our desire, the consummation of the sparrow's
wings" (p. 163). But the oxymoron "mournful frolic"
indicates another side, as does the image of a crucifixion.
Michael has been redeemed—Sydney Slyter tells us that
too—he has taken some action to gain control of his own
life; he has been a man *"small, yet beyond elimination,
whose single presence purported a toppling of the day"*
(p. 170, my italics). In Hawkes's waste land we are all
irrevocably victims, but we can resist being victimizers,
break the chain that binds victim to victimizer (at least
in our own individual world), and temporarily halt the

cyclical reappearance of inherited terror, guilt, and desire. In that way Michael is redeemed, although the redemption and the affirmation implied in saying the individual man is "small, yet beyond elimination" is the same kind of costly symbolic affirmation characteristic of many novels in the sixties. Thus, in response to a question from an interviewer, Hawkes said of his ending: "I suppose that despite of [*sic*] all my interest in evil, all my belief in the terrifying existence of Satanism in the world, I guess by the end of that novel, I somehow intuitively must have felt the human and artistic need to arrive at a resolution which would be somehow redemptive." [6]

Where *The Lime Twig* seems especially peculiar to the sixties is in its view that something cleansing can occur in violence to allow final affirmation. Like Kesey's McMurphy and Elkin's Feldman, Michael Banks must perform a radical act in order to gain control of his life. In the waste land Hawkes has created, where memory and desire mean war and the longing for death, perhaps the only possible act of love is exorcism. In that way Michael's sacrifice is also an act of love, exorcising the power of desire; in that way the image of true lovers in the sixties is Albee's George and Martha in *Who's Afraid of Virginia Woolf?*, violently exchanging blow for blow but standing together in the end, cleansed, exorcised, and redeemed.

And after the redemption, after Michael plays the Grail Knight, "After the agony in stony places / The shouting and the crying / . . . He who was living is now dead." And the rains do come: "It was a heavy rain, the sort of rain that falls in prison yards and beats a little firewood smoke back down garret chimneys, that leaks

6. "John Hawkes on His Novels," p. 457.

across floors, into forgotten prams, into the slaughter-house and pots on the stove" (p. 173). The final scene of *The Lime Twig* makes a statement similar to the ending of Eliot's *Waste Land*. Despite the sacrifice and redemption of the individual, the waste land itself continues, for memory and desire continue. Every Michael or every Grail Knight will have to do individual battle with the internal and external forces that conspire to lay waste his world. Michael's gesture, like all symbolic gestures, does not end anything but his own dream. For Hawkes as for other novelists in the sixties the only way to move beyond the waste land is through the small individual redeeming gesture; but the waste land remains and must be confronted again and again. Others, in the pursuit of love, will dream their own unconscious dreams of death; Rock Castle will come again; and the dreamer will again terrorize himself with the shape of his dream. The victim will be as eternal as children and birds and desire. Margaret is alive at the end of the book (despite Fiedler's introduction which pronounces her dead); she lives, per-haps, as a symbol of the eternal victim, for she is carried off by Larry, Little Dora, and Thick—who begins to sweat again as he did when he first used the truncheon on her. We are left with the terror of a possible infinity of beatings.

Meanwhile, the novel ends with two detectives in the rain, somewhat comically looking for clues as if they had learned their techniques from television—looking for clues to solve the murder of Hencher. But Hencher was not murdered. He was kicked to death by Rock Castle: an accident, or another instance of love become a dream of death, he was kicked off by the creation of his own desires and guilts. The detectives' search is a masterful image of our futile attempts to make laws against a conspiracy of evil that is more internal than it is external. It is the novel's final joke—two keystone cops flailing around trying to handcuff a handful of dream. And it is the novel's final terror, for the dream is a powerful threat and the two clowns are almost all we have.

Hawkes conveys man's impotence through Sydney Slyter, the Tiresias of the book, who oversees all its action and understands the significance of Rock Castle's cyclical reappearance, but is powerless to alter the race. Like Tiresias, Slyter is a prophet who has "perceived the scene and foretold the rest"—his comments preface every chapter, appearing like prophecies to tell us what will come next. But the voice of the prophet is powerless in the waste land, and Sydney Slyter is another version of Hawkes's victim, another bird on a lime twig, recalling Eliot's use of birds to symbolize the voiceless impotence of the poet-prophet. His newspaper columns stand by themselves; they have no effect on the action of the novel, so Slyter's warnings about Rock Castle and the evils involved go unheeded. All that is left is his weary knowledge and his questions—"What now of Sydney Slyter's view of the world? What now of my prognostications?" (p. 140).

The question is the same as Eliot's question: what could be the role of the artist in the waste land world? Hawkes's answer could speak for many of the black humor fabulists of the sixties:

> If the true purpose of the novel is to assume a significant shape and to objectify the terrifying similarity between the unconscious desires of the solitary man and the disruptive needs of the visible world; then the satiric writer, running maliciously at the head of the mob and creating the shape of his meaningful

psychic paradox as he goes, will serve best the novel's purpose. . . . I too believe very much in the sack of the past slung around our necks, in all the recurrent ancestral fear and abortive birth we find in dreams as well as literature. The constructed vision, the excitement of the undersea life of the inner man, a language appropriate to the delicate malicious knowledge of us all as poor, forked, corruptible, the feeling of pleasure and pain that comes when something pure and contemptible lodges in the imagination—I believe in the "singular and terrible attraction" of all this. For me the writer should always serve as his own angleworm— and the sharper the barb with which he fishes himself out of the blackness, the better.[7]

The constructed vision, extreme and violent in order to assure us that fiction and fantasy are not only mingled with fact, but are distinguishable only because the artist has made his construction obvious—the constructed vision that seeks to understand the mystery of fact and the mystery of the solitary man—this is the vision of the fabulist in the sixties, the Tiresias as Fisher King who uses his fable to fish himself out of the blackness. The fable is the form for the constructed vision; it is the form many contemporary writers use to help make art from our lost faith in the distinction between fact and fiction; it is the form that enables the writer to move beyond the bleak vision of the waste land. For most writers of the sixties are not world-weary wastelanders rehearsing a ritual of despair—they are men anxious to affirm life no matter what the cost; they are men whose greatest fear is that the world has grown weary of itself

7. "Notes on the Wild Goose Chase," *Massachusetts Review* 3 (Summer 1962): 787–88.

and begun to pursue its death. So they have turned the terror of a world where fact and fiction blur into fables whose "barbs" paradoxically offer a slim hope of redemption—a hope "small, yet beyond elimination." Speaking of Michael's sacrifice when he stops the race at the end of *The Lime Twig*, Hawkes quipped:

> Oddly enough, I thought I was doing something absolutely impossible, improbable, in that action. But a friend of mine gave me a newspaper clipping, not long ago, about the fact that in the 125th running of the Derby in England—in that race, just such an accident occurred. And all of the horses fell down on the field and the jockeys were left sprawling limp on the field and this scene was right out of a novel. I was very pleased that life does imitate fiction.[8]

THE LIGHTER SIDE OF CONSPIRACY: A NOTE ON
STANLEY ELKIN'S *Boswell*

There is another way to deal with what Hawkes calls "the terrifying similarity between the unconscious desires of the solitary man and the disruptive needs of the visible world." It is to emphasize solitude itself—to point to our long-established knowledge that man is trapped in himself, unable to move beyond the circle of his own limited experience, and tyrannized by the demands of the same impenetrable self that is the cause of his solitude. The self's tyranny is one way of explaining the force that has gained control over the life of the individual; and the individual's enforced solitude can explain his construction of external conspiracies; hearing only vague echoes and seeing only dim shadows, the in-

8. "John Hawkes on His Novels," p. 457.

dividual can be convinced that something is going on, something which must by its very exclusion of him be a demonic plot against him. There is a good joke in all this which has made the somewhat traditional theme of the self's solitude attractive to black humorists in the sixties: it is a theme that turns our preoccupation with conspiracies back upon us, claiming that the real conspirators are our own isolated and tyrannical selves. This is a simplification that denies even the collusion between external events and the self which is Hawkes's version of conspiracy. Since it blames everything on the internal world, it is the other side of the response that finds all the devils in the external world.

Although the theme of the isolated self does offer one more argument—a traditional one—to the ongoing dialogue about the powers that rule us, it is usually treated with comparative lightness by the writer in the sixties. Perhaps its open simplification of our conflicts and the very fact that it is a traditional answer has made the joke more fascinating than the suffering usually connected with the self's isolation and its tyrannical demands. This kind of emphasis on the comic side of conspiracy and the human ego appears in books like *Boswell* by Stanley Elkin, *Reinhart in Love* by Thomas Berger, *The Moviegoer* and *The Last Gentleman* by Walker Percy, *The Player King* by Earl Rovit, and even to some extent *The Sot-Weed Factor* by John Barth. While the poignancy of human isolation is not lost on these writers, the theme itself undergoes some variations that make its appearance different from what it has been in the past. For instance: isolation does not result in deep introspective despair; although the self and the ego end up as the ultimate cause of man's miseries, the blurring of fact and fiction is still acknowledged, for a fabulous world is depicted as an extension of man's fabulous ego; the passive hero—who is characteristic of those novels in the sixties that deal with conspiracy—becomes a voyeur, a kind of outsider whose passivity is somewhere between the passivity of Thomas Pynchon's inert characters and that of the more traditional sufferer of isolation, as in, say, William Styron's *Lie Down in Darkness*; despite this brand of passivity and despite the heavy burden of blame that falls on the individual self, the vital necessity of affirming life continues to be primary. Curiously enough, the writer in the sixties uses the theme of isolation in a way that resembles the techniques of Hawthorne and Melville more than it resembles those of some twentieth-century writers; perhaps only the emphasis on the comic separates the real literary response to isolation in the sixties from the response in *The Scarlet Letter*.

Stanley Elkin's *Boswell* demonstrates clearly and very amusingly how the theme of the self's isolation has been made a usable property for the black humorist in the sixties.[9] Boswell, the major character, the king of voyeurs, tells us that "demeaning introspection leads nowhere," that the business of life is to keep on living—and so in full recognition of his isolation and of his voracious ego, he embraces life, and pursues the living of it in mad comic desperation. His goal is simply to have every experience and to know everything everyone is thinking; he dreams of literally forming a "Club" for all the "Great" men of the world and then forcing each of them to tell him all their impressions while he tells them his, and they tell him theirs of his, et cetera. His life is a comic version of Eliot's lines from "What the

9. Page numbers for all citations from *Boswell* will be included parenthetically in the text.

Thunder Said" in *The Waste Land*: "We think of the key, each in his prison / Thinking of the key, each confirms a prison." Thus, Boswell spends his life knocking on doors and gate-crashing frantically on the Famous and the Great, but no matter what door he knocks on or what gate he crashes, he only finds passage into one more chamber of the self. Since he finds gate-crashing better than selflessness and better than submissiveness, he turns in earnest to being a voyeur. But, he is no simply passive peeping-tom, and although he tells us, "I have heard the stewardesses singing each to each. I do not think that they will sing to me," he is no jet-age J. Alfred Prufrock either. He is out to live, and he pours a great deal of passion into bringing the Great together in a meeting of "The Club."

Boswell's life ultimately demonstrates the paradox that the self's hunger and its demands really do lay waste our lives, and yet to suffer from isolation and selfishness is to be human and alive. Like Pynchon's characters and Hawkes's characters, Boswell recognizes that even love is limited in helping man escape the prison of the self, for "the weight of one's solitary existence was overwhelming; one was pinned by it, caged by it like an animal. (Surely . . . love is only the effort weak men put forth to compromise their solitariness)" (p. 370). Yet, Boswell, a man of the sixties, is willing gleefully to embrace even solitude, selfishness, and isolation if that is what it costs to live and be human—and not just embrace, but celebrate the joke that his life is a "sad extravagance," yet a life nonetheless.

There is no search for identity in Boswell's life; there is only a rapid expansion of his ego's demands and a recognition of that expansion. Boswell denies the very basis of the idea that the self can voyage in search of discovery, for "Boswell is Boswell. His truth is that the personality is simply another name for habit and that what we view as a fresh decision is only a rededication, a new way to get old things; that the evolving self is an illusion, fate just some final consequence" (p. 228). As a man grows older, Boswell claims, either he becomes more obsessed or he allows his life to become complex, which means he undergoes a "diminishment of passion." The great thing for Boswell is to be obsessed, to maintain his certainties, because any diminishment, self-containment, selflessness, or martyrhood is a denial of self and therefore a denial of life and humanity. His obsession is, of course, to engineer a gathering of the Great for a meeting of The Club. And he succeeds.

Through The Club, Boswell hopes (somewhat unconsciously at first) to be the voyeur who absorbs everything and everyone into his own self, thereby coming to know them, be them, be the world and live forever. The joke and the ugliness of such an absurd plan is revealed in Boswell's dream just before The Club does have its meeting. He dreams that he uses the meeting to make everyone reveal all their thoughts to him, and when that fails, he actually begins to absorb everyone, literally filling the room,

> forcing the others to flee into corners, pressing them hopelessly against the walls. . . . As they suffocated and died they began to shrink also and so made more room. . . . I was greater than the room now and expanding into the street itself, where the crowds fell back from me as they would from a tidal wave. There was no place for them to go, and soon I had taken their space as I had taken the others' before. And still I continued to grow. Whole populations were plunged

into a stifling darkness in the shadow of my calves. Races dived into my pockets and no sooner had found room there than my thighs, swelling, smothered them against the lining. Gradually the cries of the stricken began to subside, their great grief silent only when there were no more mourners. "Ah," I said, my voice like thunder in the surrounding silence, "a way had to be found, and a way *was* found!" [p. 380]

Boswell is frightened by his dream, and when he actually goes to the meeting of The Club he falsifies his name and is denied entrance. He is trapped by the central dilemma of the book, by the black joke at the core of his vision—to enter The Club is to totally indulge his ego, to risk *giving* the self the power it needs to destroy life; to stay outside is to abandon his obsession and *allow* the death of the self. Boswell settles back in the crowd that surrounds the meeting place, "peacefully with others. The self at rest, the ego sleeping, death unremembered for once" (p. 386). Yet, how can the self have peace without death? How can Boswell put his ego to rest without diminishing his passionate and vital zest for life, without becoming less than human in his own eyes? "But what's this, what's this?" Boswell asks the moment after he pronounces the sleep of the self, "What am I thinking of? The ego, the ego. Sleeping. Say, I thought, who was I kidding?" Boswell seizes upon the final joke; holding fast to both horns of his dilemma, he speaks as an artist, a creator—The Club, after all, is his creation, his fable; and if his ego brought it into being and found it to be a monster, his ego can destroy it and still stay alive—he speaks as a human being transcending his dilemma through the fabulist's symbolic gesture: "Hey,

hey, down with The Club," he shouts, "Down with The Club. *Down with The Club.*"

If Thomas Pynchon hinted at the possibility of an external conspiracy, Elkin's Boswell dismisses that possibility: that is, he dismisses it if we are willing to believe in his world, if we are willing to embrace both selfishness and the very self that conspires against us—if we are willing to believe that celebrating the conspiracy of the insatiable ego is the only way to live as a passionate human being. In a sense, because the joke of our victimization is on us (the victimizers), Boswell, by asking us to embrace the self's solitude even if it is the only cause of conspiracy, is asking us not just to understand the black humorist's vision of life's sad extravagance, but to *be* black humorists ourselves, and celebrate life itself, embracing the black joke of it all. If we are puzzled by the strange shape of the resulting reality, we may ask along with Boswell, "What the hell *isn't* reality; who doesn't face up to it?" This may be the only real moral-at-the-end-of-the-tale which the fabulists of the sixties would agree upon.

If, as both Hawkes and Elkin suggest, Conspiracy is, at least in part, an internal thing, then perhaps our fear of having lost power over our own lives to some conspiracy can only be dealt with by exorcism. If we do not exorcise the fear, then all we can do is wait with Pynchon's Oedipa Maas to see if conspiracy really exists, or stand outside some "Club" with Boswell, yelling at a rumored conspiracy that we know we ourselves have created. In any case, we seem to be stuck forever on the outside looking in, hoping to glimpse some way of dealing with whatever power rules over us.

In every novel I have discussed, with the possible exception of *One Flew over the Cuckoo's Nest,* any hope of moving beyond the waste land or feeling assured we control our own lives has been entirely a contrived construct of the imagination; and if—as we have seen repeatedly in these novels—man dreams a dream of annihilation in one form or another while his only comforting act of love is to exorcise that dream, then the contrived construction of the fable is the *author's* act of love. For the fable, by the mere act of containing the horrors of the waste land in a form that contradicts its content— a form usually connected with happy endings—exorcises those horrors. The strange mixture of the fabulist's love with the black humorist's dark impulse to exorcise has led critics to compare the black humor fable with Swiftian satire, but the comparison needs qualifying, for the spirit and the tone are very different from Swift's. The black humor fabulist includes his own sins with his reader's sins and, therefore, never chastises from a superior position. This is one of his favorite jokes: his impulse to exorcise is armed timidly with the gentle fable form and not meant to flay us with the scourge of chastisement.

The fable should comfort and humanize at all costs by prodding us awake from our fearful dream of annihilation, and the black humor should pain and delight while it pictures us all trapped in the same waste land, all guilty of the same kind of dream. In the world of the black humor fable, exorcism *is* comfort, and the gentle fable *is* a prod. Why *not* call that world a black joke?—a place where killers slap each other around with fable-feathered pillows, or jokers play patty-cake with big, very deadly weapons; a place where all of us, including the author, are dark vaudevillians, killer clowns.

Even when the black humor fabulist includes a moral to his fable, it always has the ring of confession and not chastisement, as with Kurt Vonnegut, Jr., who constantly reminds us that any one of us could be as nazi as the next, and no one can really play judge-at-nuremberg. To prepare ourselves for the final move to fable land, we might look at the moral Vonnegut frames for the preface to *Mother Night*—a moral which could preface a great many of the fables we have already seen, emphasizing the fabulist's confessional inclusion of himself among those who need exorcism, the black humorist's reluctance to affirm any virtuous absolutes beyond the value of life over death, and the humanist's desire to make love serve him as both an exorcism and an affirmation.

> If I'd been born in Germany, I suppose I would have *been* a Nazi, bopping Jews and gypsies and Poles around, leaving boots sticking out of snowbanks, warming myself with my secretly virtuous insides. So it goes.
>
> There's another clear moral to this tale, now that I think about it: When you're dead you're dead.
>
> And yet another moral occurs to me now: Make love when you can. It's good for you. [p. vii]

PART III: FROM WASTE LAND TO FABLE LAND

The two authors I have reserved for this last section are more recognizable as fabulists than the authors I have discussed to this point. Kurt Vonnegut, Jr., and Peter S. Beagle are among the best writers of the sixties and they represent a full spectrum of the possibilities offered by the fable form. The difference between their works and, say, *V.* or *The Lime Twig* as regards the use of the fable, and even in terms of vision, is largely a matter of degree. They are both willing to let some traditional devices of the fable stick out—allegory and didacticism, for example. The one essential difference, perhaps, is their use of exorcism, which often comes closer to the Greek concept of catharsis than to Hawkes's violent cleansing: they see love as an act of exorcism rather than exorcism as an act of love, and in that difference lies the deep sense of humane tenderness in their novels.

The fable's ability to contain our terror by enclosing our agonies with the expectation of a happy ending and by giving us hope of some distance on our dilemmas makes it, perhaps, the key literary instrument in the sixties for moving beyond the waste land. More writers than I am able to discuss have used the fable with a sense of its relevance to our times (see my bibliography for a list of related fables). Those of us who still feel that the black humorists and fabulists talk about a world unrecognizable—and that seems to be the main complaint of reviewers—should consider the following comments by Larry L. King which preface a review of a political history book, *An American Melodrama: The Presidential Campaign of 1968:*

> The America of 1968, with its assassinations, torched ghettos, campus wars, crime waves, alienations, deposed kings and crazed pretenders, almost seems too much for a single book. Offered as a novel, it might be rejected even by the lowliest of publishing house read-

ers. "This story smacks too much of fantasy," such a
low-echelon reader might report to his superiors.
"There is too much random violence, nameless com-
plications, and wild improbabilities. The Southern
Governor known as George Wallace is surely over-
drawn; a composite of all the Dixie demagogues of the
past. That his racist appeals could enjoy enough popular support to get his name on ballots in virtually
all states, through the signing of petitions by millions,
is incredible. That he would name a Stone Age primi-
tive from the military ranks as his running mate caps
incredibility with foolhardiness. The aging Hollywood
idol who has somehow become governor of California
(!) and who within two years can reach for the Presidency, is more a satirical figure than not: I cannot determine whether we are meant to take him seriously.
The young prince figure, Senator Robert Kennedy,
dies so senseless and near-accidental a death in his moment of triumph . . . that only the most amateurish
novelist would dare present it. [*New Republic,* 31 May
1969, pp. 24–25.]

And so it goes. The fable seems almost a necessary form
if we expect both fidelity to our sense of contemporary
experience and some distinction between fact and fiction
—if we expect some response other than Norman Mailer's "History as a Novel, the Novel as History." We may
even need to go to Tralfamadore with Vonnegut or listen
to a unicorn with Beagle in order, finally, to get the kind
of perspective on fact which would allow us to say—as
one of Elkin's reviewers did say—something as com-
fortable as, "That doesn't sound like the world I live
in."

7: OUT OF THE WASTE LAND
AND INTO THE FIRE:
CATACLYSM OR THE COSMIC COOL

No novelist in the sixties is more aware of the necessity of exorcising our dreams of death than Kurt Vonnegut, Jr., and no novelist is more avid in his use of the fable form as an exorcising comfort and a loving gentle prod. The dark, tough, apocalyptic quality of Vonnegut's vision results from his hard-minded recognition that we do commit sins against ourselves which need to be exorcised. But he dresses that perception in the fable's soft fabric, moral fibers and all, because he sees love as the proper instrument of exorcism, and the fable as the proper form for the expression of the artist's love. " 'All these years,' " exclaims one of his characters, Kilgore Trout, a sometime science-fiction fabulist, savior, and surrogate for Vonnegut, " 'All these years,' he says, 'I've been opening the window and making love to the world.' " [1] Vonnegut's fables have morals and they expose

1. *Slaughterhouse-Five or The Children's Crusade,* p. 145. Page numbers for all further citations will be included parenthetically in the text. The abbreviation *SLF* will be used when necessary to distinguish this from other Vonnegut novels.

sins—the morals usually are simple admonishments to love, and the sins are one variety of pride or another. The universe he pictures is indifferent to man and man spends his time trying to twist that indifference into order and meaning. The fable is an appropriate form for Vonnegut because it requires a certain willing suspension of disbelief in order for us to go on reading, and Vonnegut believes we need that same kind of suspension in order to go on living in a world dominated by science, slaughter, and an infinite number of irresponsible everyday atrocities. Like Pynchon, he finds we have exhausted our values and can go on living only through the acceptance of illusions. We need illusions not to escape life but to deal with it, and what better form for the author's gift of an illusion than the fable.

By using the fable, Vonnegut is able to create an illusion whose moral is that we should create illusions; thus we have a fable called *Cat's Cradle* about a religion called Bokononism made up of "harmless untruths," which, nonetheless, ideally offers comfort to its believers even while it tells them it is all an illusion.[2] Vonnegut would have his fable function just as Bokononism does, encompassing "the cruel paradox of Bokononist thought, the heartbreaking necessity of lying about reality, and the heartbreaking impossibility of lying about it" (*CC*, p. 229). I believe this accounts for the strange dark joke in Vonnegut's work: we are given an array of illusions to live by, but can make no use of them, for how can an illusion be anything but an illusion if we are conscious that it *is* one? We cannot live by Bokononism, and indeed *Cat's Cradle* ends with a cataclysm; we can only echo

2. Page numbers for all citations from *Cat's Cradle* will be included parenthetically in the text. The abbreviation *CC* will be used when necessary to distinguish this from other Vonnegut novels.

Eliot Rosewater, who, appearing for a second time in Vonnegut's work, tells a psychiatrist in *Slaughterhouse-Five*, "I think you are going to have to come up with a lot of wonderful new lies, or people just aren't going to want to go on living" (*SLF*, pp. 87–88). The final dark implication, which Vonnegut shares with a great many other writers, is that we too are headed for cataclysm unless we find something to live by. Vonnegut does offer two possibilities—we can learn to love each other, or we can each create our own illusion, some mythology that will help us learn to live together. Neither possibility makes life meaningful, but both do offer a way to stay alive, and maybe even have some fun.

The particular power of Vonnegut's work—especially in the four books which develop his distinctive voice, all published in the sixties—is in the deceptively simple way he deals with the extraordinary nature of contemporary fact. Vonnegut is a master at getting inside a cliché and tilting it enough off center to reveal both the horror and the mystery that lies beneath the surface of the most placidly dull and ordinary human response. I will, I hope, be able to show some of that, but I will be primarily concerned with discussing the moral vision in Vonnegut's fables: the world man lives in; how he lives; the good illusions or morals to the tale; and the bad illusions or sins. These kinds of concerns are central to Vonnegut's work, because more than any other writer I have dealt with, he wants us to hear his message. For the sake of that message he sometimes sacrifices literary fullness—that is, he will tell us his point instead of showing us. He will sometimes juxtapose historical fact and his own fiction without running them through any very complete imaginative transformation, as in his use of Harry Truman's announcement of the dropping of the

atom bomb in *Slaughterhouse-Five*. We should read
Vonnegut with some different criteria; if we grant that
he has designs upon us and that he sometimes sacrifices
fictive device for absolute clarity, often sounding more
like a social scientist than a novelist, then we can forget
his occasional failure to justify the literary tradition he
half evokes, and judge him on the genuine quality of a
passionately honest heart and mind working over the
bewildering facts of contemporary experience. In that
light he can be unusually poignant and moving. He is
brilliant at the honed-down black joke which speaks for
itself and he is equally brilliant at the kind of blatant
social didacticism that speaks for the author. " 'I've worried some about why write books, when Presidents and
Senators and generals do not read them,' he says, 'and
the university experience taught me a very good reason:
you catch people before they become generals and Senators and Presidents, and you *poison their minds with
humanity*. Encourage them to make a better world.' " [3]

Man, according to Vonnegut, makes a waste land of
his life by looking for some meaningful absolute purpose instead of simply living. Although Vonnegut's tone,
spirit, and overall response to man are very different
from Jonathan Swift's, his idea of the universe and man's
role in it is somewhat Swiftian, for he pictures us as modern Lilliputians, claiming big things for ourselves in a
universe too immense to be anything but indifferent.
His answer to the question of what power has gained
control over our lives varies from book to book; on the
whole, men are "the listless playthings of enormous
forces." We might, perhaps, be controlled by strange

3. From an interview with C. D. B. Bryan; see "Kurt Vonnegut,
Head Bokononist," *New York Times Book Review,* 6 Apr. 1969, p.
2 (Vonnegut's italics).

creatures that look like "plumber's friends," from the planet Tralfamadore, who have used us to transmit messages to one of their space travelers stranded on the planet Titan with an ailing spaceship. This would mean our history has been entirely controlled by these creatures who are rushing a spare part to their stranded man: "The meaning of Stonehenge in Tralfamadorian, when viewed from above, is: 'Replacement part being rushed with all possible speed.'"; or "The Great Wall of China means in Tralfamadorian, when viewed from above: 'Be patient. We haven't forgotten about you.'" [4] While we scheme in our puny way about our grand purposes, we are really only instruments for the delivery of a spare part to a space traveler who is on his way to another galaxy to deliver a message which says only: "Greetings." The point, as it always is when Vonnegut takes us to another planet, is to give us some perspective on man's pride, so that we can quit worrying about how we fit into cosmic purpose and start worrying about how we can be kind to each other. (If there is any doubt that Vonnegut is a fabulist in the mainstream of the sixties and not a science fiction writer, his own definition of science fiction should end that doubt, for he sees its fantasies as revealing "an impossibly hospitable world"—no one could say the same of Vonnegut's world.)

Other forces that have gained control over us (besides the possibility of Tralfamadorians) are: money—*God Bless You, Mr. Rosewater*; our own nearsightedness—*Cat's Cradle*; and Governments—*Mother Night*. In his latest novel, *Slaughterhouse-Five or The Children's Cru-*

4. *The Sirens of Titan*, p. 271. Page numbers for all further citations will be included parenthetically in the text. The abbreviation *ST* will be used when necessary to distinguish this from other Vonnegut novels.

sade, Vonnegut blurs all these forces into a single sense
of timeless determinism that resembles the Greek concept of Fate. Billy Pilgrim, the main character, is a traveler in time and learns (from the Tralfamadorians again)
that time is a continuum, not a series of separate moments. Thus, his life and his death have existed always
and will exist always. Because he can be a traveler in
time, he can visit any moment in his life; he can glimpse
the whole thing like a chain of mountains; he can pick
his favorite moments and look at them, for they have
always been there and always will be there. Ultimately,
this is not so delightful as it sounds—as Billy discovers,
man's moments are usually pretty lousy. Such a vision
of destiny is the one Bokonon preaches in *Cat's Cradle*
—things do not just happen; they happen as they are
supposed to happen. Bokonon, of course, would admit
that this theory of fate is really an illusion, but it is a
good illusion if it teaches us to stop committing hubris,
to stop using up our lives in speculation about wide
forces and big powers, so we can improve the simple
quality of life and perhaps avoid self-annihilation in the
name of Purpose and Meaning. It is a bad illusion if it
leads to grand-scale indifference and to utter passivity
as it does in Billy Pilgrim who is a walking dead man,
a man whose only intimation of humanity is that he is
forced to take naps because he finds himself weeping for
no apparent reason. Vonnegut does not attempt to really
explain the question of fate as some conjunction of external and internal forces or some mysterious conspiracy,
as Pynchon and Hawkes do; he is closer to the Greeks
because he frowns on the question itself as something
irrelevant to the human sphere, an unknowable and ultimately unprofitable question to dwell on. But Vonnegut's

rationale for such a concept of fate is different from the Greek: we *need not* ask about the powers that rule and the meaning of life because life is meaningless; we *should not* ask because the question misplaces emphasis and makes us wonder about Meaning—it makes us take part in "Children's Crusades" to prove one theory of meaning better than any other, and generally wreak havoc on one another. Once we discard all notions that life is meaningful or purposeful, we can turn to each other and recognize as Bokonon does that purposeful or not the only thing sacred is man.

As I pointed out in the Introduction, Vonnegut is close to Melville in his vision of man's place in the cosmos—he indicates his awareness of this similarity in the opening line of *Cat's Cradle,* "Call me Jonah"—for he too asks us to lower our "conceit of attainable felicity," to concentrate on the quality of life and not our importance in the scheme of things, and most of all to share the thump on the back that life hands out. If there was a Creation, and God did spend any time on it, Vonnegut assures us through Bokonon that it must have gone like this:

> In the beginning, God created the earth, and he looked upon it in His cosmic loneliness.
> And God said, "Let Us make living creatures out of mud, so the mud can see what We have done." And God created every living creature that now moveth, and one was man. Mud as man alone could speak. God leaned close as mud as man sat up, looked around, and spoke. Man blinked. "What is the *purpose* of all this?" he asked politely.
> "Everything must have a purpose?" asked God.

"Certainly," said man.

"Then I leave it to you to think of one for all this," said God. And He went away. [*CC,* pp. 214–15]

Because of our pride and bad illusions—which are the dragons in Vonnegut's fables—the quality of human life as he presents it is horrendous. The way we live influences the dark part of Vonnegut's vision, for, as Howard W. Campbell, Jr., puts it in *Mother Night,* anyone growing up in this world expecting peace and order will "be eaten alive." The texture of our lives is made clearest in *Slaughterhouse-Five*—a title that ostensibly refers to a real meat slaughterhouse in Dresden, but which reflects a sense of our world at its worst. When the Tralfamadorians tell Billy Pilgrim in *Slaughterhouse-Five* to live the way they do and ignore life's ugly moments, Vonnegut juxtaposes this advice with some of Billy's childhood moments: a trip to the Grand Canyon and one to Carlsbad Caverns—both are moments filled with fear, terror, and flirtation with death. The world he lives in does not offer Billy too many marvelous moments at all; the tone is set by World War II, by prison camps and prison trains, by incredible hatred between men—allies and enemies both—and finally by the outrageous fire-bomb destruction of Dresden. This is the moment that Vonnegut himself keeps coming back to, a moment he actually witnessed as a prisoner of war; it is the personal basis of the apocalyptic darkness in his vision, for if man is capable of a senseless and absolutely gratuitous slaughter like Dresden, then he is capable of total world destruction. At the end of *Cat's Cradle* the world is virtually destroyed by a doomsday invention called *ice-nine*—the weapon of destruction is unimportant; Vonnegut's concern is not that we have finally equipped ourselves with weapons big enough to make a world wide Dresden, but that we are capable of the kind of inhumanity that leads to moments like Dresden, Hiroshima, Auschwitz, and so on. These are the moments that define Vonnegut's world and appear constantly throughout his work, making his fables the same kind of mixture of fact and fiction that we saw in Pynchon, Elkin, Hawkes, and Heller. It is a world where fact has become so fabulous that Howard W. Campbell, Jr., in *Mother Night* cannot successfully write unbelievable propaganda—no matter how absurd he gets, no matter how insanely he pictures things, people believe him and find his fictions as good as facts: "I had hoped, as a broadcaster, to be merely ludicrous," he tells us, "but this is a hard world to be ludicrous in, with so many human beings so reluctant to laugh, so incapable of thought, so eager to believe and snarl and hate." [5]

Slaughterhouse-Five goes the furthest of all Vonnegut's books in mixing fact with fiction. "All this happened, more or less," he tells us on the first page, and the voice of the narrator in the first chapter is decidedly and openly Vonnegut speaking about Vonnegut. The body of the book tells the story of Billy Pilgrim, a fictional someone who was at Dresden with Vonnegut the narrator. Billy too is clearly a ghost in Vonnegut's chamber of fears about himself. Billy has been deadened by his experience and is passive to the slaughters he continues to witness—to an airplane crash that kills everyone on board but himself; to Vietnam and his son, who, we are told repeatedly, has been straightened out by the Green

5. *Mother Night*, p. 120. Page numbers for all further citations will be included parenthetically in the text. The abbreviation *MN* will be used when necessary to distinguish this from other Vonnegut novels.

Berets; to his wife's death and to his own death. Clearly, Billy can afford to be a little passive since he is "unstuck in time" and knows the past, the present, and the future. But the detached cool he develops obviously is too detached for Vonnegut the narrator, who in contrast tells us of himself:

> I have told my sons that they are not under any circumstances to take part in massacres, and that the news of massacres of enemies is not to fill them with satisfaction or glee.
>
> I have also told them not to work for companies which make massacre machinery, and to express contempt for people who think we need machinery like that. [*SLF*, p. 17]

There is, however, something about Billy's detachment that is attractive to Vonnegut. As narrator he too tries a small touch of it—a kind of *cosmic cool* that comes with looking at himself from some perspective, from an interplanetary vantage point, perhaps. In Vonnegut's novels a little cosmic cool, if it does not turn into indifference, helps some of his characters resist Lilliputian pride. It helps them cool off a little about their own deaths. Vonnegut has a running symbol for that kind of detachment—it appears in *Cat's Cradle, God Bless You, Mr. Rosewater,* and *Slaughterhouse-Five,* and is reminiscent of a symbol used by John Hawkes. Hovering above the abyss of total destruction, reminding us that there is little to say about massacres, and nothing to say about Purpose and Meaning, Vonnegut continually pictures a small bird asking eternally a small question: "Poo-tee-weet?" If such a question means anything, it probably means "so what"; but it also means "I see the dimensions of human life and I survive!"

A second device Vonnegut uses to convey a sense of proportion about the world he sees is the phrase "so it goes," which he uses after every mention of death in *Slaughterhouse-Five*. The death of a dog, of Christ, of a fictional character, of the bubbles in champagne, of 135,-000 Germans and 6,000,000 Jews, of Robert Kennedy, of Martin Luther King, and of narrator-Vonnegut's father all rate the same response—"so it goes." Death of any kind is meaningless and all deaths are equal—Vonnegut tells us the term comes from the Tralfamadorians whose perspective on time allows them to see death as just another moment in life.

> "When a Tralfamadorian sees a corpse, all he thinks is that the dead person is in bad condition in that particular moment, but that the same person is just fine in plenty of other moments. Now, when I myself hear that somebody is dead, I simply shrug and say what the Tralfamadorians say about dead people, which is 'So it goes.' " [*SLF*, p. 23]

This kind of cosmic cool is of course an illusion, but as Vonnegut warns us, if we are to keep our heads and continue to live while we are looking into the abyss of possible cataclysm, we are going to have to learn some new lies—we are going to have to learn to say "Poo-tee-weet?" and "so it goes." It is what the fabulist says by containing his black vision in a form we usually connect with happy endings; it is what the black humorist says when he is laughing; it is very much the imagistic counterpart of what Pynchon says when he tells us "to keep cool but care." It is not said without compassion. If I

may continue to use the term *cosmic cool,* I think it can
help us understand the ideal way to live in Vonnegut's
world. Without it we commit personal suicide like
Howard W. Campbell, Jr., in *Mother Night,* public suicide like the cataclysm at the end of *Cat's Cradle,* spiritual suicide like Billy Pilgrim in *Slaughterhouse-Five,* or
we tear out our guts with the extraordinary efforts of
learning to care, as Eliot Rosewater does in most of
God Bless You, Mr. Rosewater. Rosewater demonstrates
that it is nearly impossible to sustain the effort it takes
to learn to care without losing our sanity, and so it is
nearly impossible to achieve the illusion of the cosmic
cool—which is made up of equal parts of love, compassion, humility, conscience, and the detached will to control these virtues and go on living no matter what. The
morals to Vonnegut's fables are hints about what illusions help achieve this happy balance, and the sins are
the villainous illusions that destroy the hope of achieving it, leaving us open in one way or another to the
ravages of destruction. We will look next at how people
do live in Vonnegut's world, their good illusions and
their bad.

Vonnegut uses the waste land image very much as
Pynchon does. His wastelanders are the same aimless,
self-seeking, potentially destructive people as Pynchon's
Whole Sick Crew, and his major characters are often
wanderers—like Pynchon's yo-yos. Vonnegut also feels,
as T. S. Eliot did, that only the restoration of some mythology can move man beyond the waste land. But, as
always, there is a dark joke involved, for Vonnegut's
mythologies and religions are contrived and obvious illusions, not the holy words of a truly felt religion. Yet,
there is still another turn to the joke; his illusions are
meant to help teach us how to love and actually do move

some of his characters beyond the sterility of the waste land. Where they go depends on both the quality of their illusions and how well they learn the lessons of love; the choices are: cataclysm, or life and the cosmic cool.

The archetype for Vonnegut's constructed mythologies appears in *The Sirens of Titan*; it is called "The Church of God the Utterly Indifferent," and its key precept is "Take Care of the People and God Almighty Will Take Care of Himself." Bokononism in *Cat's Cradle* is probably Vonnegut's most complete and imaginative creation of an illusionary mythology. Bokonon spends part of his time telling people that life is meaningless and man is mud, part of his time telling people they are sacred and made to be loved, and the rest assuring us that "All the true things I am about to tell you are shameless lies." Bokonon's warning is really Vonnegut's own warning about his fables, and it also informs us that "Anyone unable to understand how a useful religion can be founded on lies will not understand this book either" (*CC*, p. 16). The island of San Lorenzo—where Bokonon operates as a fugitive holy man under an agreement with the island's government to be the mythical angel-in-the-woods opposing the devil-in-the-capitol, all for the benefit of the people—this island *appears* to be a waste land, but because of Bokonon's mythology the people do share some small sense of love and spiritual comfort. The evolution of the religion clearly explains the necessity of illusion in Vonnegut's world.

> When it became evident that no governmental or economic reform was going to make the people much less miserable, the religion became the one real instrument of hope. Truth was the enemy of the people, because the truth was so terrible, so Bokonon made it his busi-

ness to provide the people with better and better lies. [*CC*, p. 143]

Many of Bokonon's lies are about how free and grand and prosperous the island of San Lorenzo is, but the major illusion is that all things happen as they are supposed to happen. People are fated to be involved in each other's lives in a predetermined way. The result is that his people do live with a certain sense of the value of the moment and the futility of worldly aspirations. Bokonon's greatest success is his influence on Mona Aamons Monzano. She is a pure creature of love, and she loves all people *uncritically,* which, as we shall see, is the way Vonnegut most approves. Mona is a personification of the love-and-compassion side of the cosmic cool, but she is unable to adopt the right sense of detachment. She says "so it goes" too willingly; she dies too easily, and her death is a clue to the biggest failure of Bokonon's illusions: since all is fated anyway, no one except the narrator and a few ugly Americans find it worthwhile to resist the spread of *ice-nine* and the destruction of life. Nor are Bokonon's lessons of love effective enough to stem the shortsightedness of the evil villain science. Frank Hoenikker, son of the father of the atom bomb—which obviously makes him brother to the bomb—substitutes abstractions and ambitions for love, and so Bokononism fails and the cataclysm comes. Frank could have married Mona—presumably a wedding of science and compassion—but he liked the scientific illusions of truth better than love. He lacked a lover's eyes:

> A lover's a liar
> To himself he lies.
> The truthful are loveless
> Like oysters their eyes. [*CC*, p. 190]

The process through which the illusion of fate can go too far and turn the cosmic cool into petrified inaction and indifference is even more clearly demonstrated during a conversation in *Slaughterhouse-Five* between Billy Pilgrim and the Tralfamadorians. Billy has just finished cataloguing some of earth's brutalities, explaining in Lilliputian-like fashion that earthlings will be the terrors of the universe and destroy everyone unless they learn peace. The Tralfamadorians tone down Billy's pride and panic with a touch of cosmic perspective, but the result is to deaden Billy's already damaged will to live instead of giving him the balanced perspective of the cosmic cool. The universe will not be destroyed by earthlings, the Tralfamadorians tell Billy:

> "We know how the universe ends"—said the guide, "and Earth has nothing to do with it, except that *it* gets wiped out, too."
> "How—how does the universe end?" said Billy.
> "We blow it up, experimenting with new fuels for our flying saucers. A Tralfamadorian test pilot presses a starter button, and the whole Universe disappears." So it goes.

> "If you know this," said Billy, "isn't there some way you can prevent it? Can't you keep the pilot from *pressing* the button?"

> "He has *always* pressed it, and he always *will*. We *always* let him and we always *will* let him. The moment is *structured* that way."

> "So—" said Billy gropingly, "I suppose that the idea of preventing war on Earth is stupid, too."
> "Of course." [*SLF*, p. 101]

It is obvious that such an illusion leads to the toleration of button pressing, and Billy's will to live is not reinforced by these Tralfamadorian insights. Bokonon himself, however, almost avoids the extremes fostered by his mythology of fate, because he is always conscious that the mythology is his own illusion, his own fable. He comes close to the posture of the cosmic cool, close enough to accept death, and still—in the middle of cataclysm—leaves advice to younger men, leaves it as he dies.

> If I were a younger man, I would write a history of human stupidity; and I would climb to the top of Mount McCabe and lie down on my back with my history for a pillow; and I would take from the ground some of the blue-white poison that makes statues of men; and I would make a statue of myself, lying on my back, grinning horribly, and thumbing my nose at You Know Who. [*CC*, p. 231]

Vonnegut is deceptively simple here, because we *do not* know "Who," nor does Bokonon. He continues making illusions right through death, pretending there is an interested Who to gesture at. The gesture is not quite the aggressive symbolic gesture of affirmation we saw in Kesey and Elkin and Heller, but it is very close to the pleasant gesture of a balanced man who has mastered the illusion of the cosmic cool—after all, what else would you do with the world all gone?

Bokonon, whose real name is Lionel Boyd Johnson— no reference to any LBJs we know, I presume—is a Negro who wanders onto San Lorenzo and almost becomes its savior. In waste land terms, he is the cured Fisher King, restoring a certain fertility to his land:

> A fish pitched up
> By the angry sea,
> I gasped on land,
> And I became me. [*CC,* p. 93]

Bokonon fails to achieve the cosmic cool because he is a little too cool, a little too detached—a mere matter of degree. At the other end of the scale Vonnegut gives us Eliot Rosewater in *God Bless You, Mr. Rosewater.* Eliot does achieve the cosmic cool in the very last moment of the book—it is Vonnegut's most affirmative book—but before that moment, Eliot is unbalanced by his extraordinary labors of love; he loses his cool, loving so intensely and so completely that he endangers his own being and loses all perspective. Eliot is a millionaire who takes up residence in the desolate town of Rosewater, Indiana, and devotes himself to the most scrupulous and vigilant responsibility toward his fellowman that could ever be conceived. Eliot's devotion to the volunteer firemen is symbol enough for Vonnegut, who tells us in another book, *The Sirens of Titan,* that "he can think of no more stirring symbol of man's humanity to man than a fire engine" (*ST,* p. 242).

Eliot becomes minutely involved with helping others, so much so that he lets his own life go entirely, loses his wife—who thinks everything Eliot is doing is beautiful, but who cannot keep his pace—takes to drink and slovenly appearance, overwhelms his father (a stereotyped conservative senator), and ends in a total breakdown. He lives a veritable orgy of human compassion. Eliot devotes himself to people who have been rejected by automation and the grind of American society; the act of love is his work of art, his illusion, his fable: "I'm go-

ing to love these discarded Americans," he tells his wife,
"even though they're useless and unattractive. *That* is
going to be my work of art." [6] For awhile his wife helps
him, and between the two of them, "They listened tire-
lessly to the misshapen fears and dreams of people who,
by almost anyone's standards, would have been better off
dead, gave them love and trifling sums of money" (p. 53).
Before Eliot cracks under the strain, he also has time to
argue with his father and express some clear-cut and
frankly preachy refutations to the antiwelfare attitude
of American political conservatives, and some very strong
indictments against the inhumanity of the profit motive.
Eliot is fully aware of the kind of people he is helping;
he is one of those rare individuals capable of entirely
"uncritical love." But it is incredibly demanding to love
and care for others every moment of your life, so Eliot
does indeed crack up. His crack-up, however, is not
entirely the result of the exertions of love—he is also
hounded by some certain memories of the destruction of
Dresden, and by his father's attitude toward him. Eliot
decidedly loses the detached perspective necessary for the
posture of the cosmic cool, but he does excel in the love,
compassion, and conscience side of that ideal balance.
In the closing pages of the book Vonnegut trots out
Kilgore Trout—deus-ex-fabula—to explain the significance of Eliot's uncritical love, and, incidentally, to explain the significance of the fabulist's loving gift of his
art:

> "It's news that a man was able to *give* that kind of
> love over a long period of time. If one man can do it,

6. *God Bless You, Mr. Rosenwater, or Pearls before Swine,* p. 47.
Page numbers for all further citations will be included parenthetically in the text. The abbreviation *GBMR* will be used when
necessary to distinguish this from other Vonnegut novels.

perhaps others can do it, too. It means that our hatred of useless human beings and the cruelties we inflict upon them for their own good need not be parts of human nature. Thanks to the example of Eliot Rosewater, millions upon millions of people may learn to love and help whomever they see." [p. 213]

Vonnegut seems to be saying that Eliot Rosewater makes it possible to believe all men are capable not only of moments like Dresden and Auschwitz, but also capable of really giving and really sympathizing. In Eliot Rosewater we can see the close relationship between Vonnegut's implied concept of the cosmic cool, and T. S. Eliot's formula: give, sympathize, and control—Rosewater's name might not be Eliot for nothing. Until the end of the book Eliot Rosewater is able to give and sympathize, but only at the cost of self-control, or at the cost of the cosmic balanced detachment that Vonnegut sees necessary for the maintenance of life. But Rosewater's final gesture achieves that ideal balance; it is that same kind of symbolic gesture of affirmation we have seen to be characteristic of many novels in the sixties, and it is also, I believe, a beautiful and moving moment in Vonnegut's own response to human possibilities. Rosewater, in an asylum, suddenly comes out of the mental and spiritual stupor that had fallen on him when he ended his efforts in Rosewater, Indiana. Regaining his mental balance, he learns that his entire fortune is in danger because an obscure branch of the family can take it away on the basis of his apparent insanity. Eliot also learns that fifty-six women, out of some strange sense of love, have claimed that he fathered their children. The obscure relatives—the Rhode Island Rosewaters—were going to use this as a proof of Eliot's unbalanced charac-

ter, but when the number rose to fifty-six they abandoned the plan as too ludicrous. Eliot learns of the pa-
ternity claims just as he comes back to his senses, and he
realizes that having an heir would save his fortune from
the greedy relatives. In a magnificent final gesture he
adopts all fifty-six heirs—all fifty-six useless misfits born
from useless parents. He achieves the perfect balance of
the cosmic cool: sitting in his tennis clothes, tennis racket
in hand, he looks up into a tree and hears the magic
question "Poo-tee-weet?" and he turns to tell his lawyer
and his father:

> "I now instruct you to draw up at once papers that will
> legally acknowledge that every child in Rosewater
> County said to be mine is mine, regardless of blood
> type. Let them all have full rights of inheritance as
> my sons and daughters."
>
> "Eliot!"
>
> "Let their names be Rosewater from this moment
> on. And tell them that their father loves them, no
> matter what they turn out to be. And tell them—" Eliot
> fell silent, raised his tennis racket as though it were
> a magic wand.
>
> "And tell them," he began again "to be fruitful and
> multiply." [p. 217]

Vonnegut has no better symbol of the ideal way to live in
the world he sees as ours.

Vonnegut's man most unsuccessful at living in the
world is Howard W. Campbell, Jr., in *Mother Night*.
Campbell was a double agent during World War II—
an American writing and broadcasting Nazi propaganda
in Germany that really relayed secret messages to America. But he was too good at the propaganda, turning his
imagination and his art—he once wrote plays about love

and Grail Knights—to some of the most scurrilous hate documents ever written. He may have really lost himself, lost in his double identity, in a crazy world of war, but whoever he was when he wrote the propaganda, "he was one of the most vicious sons of bitches who ever lived" (p. 138). Even a high-ranking German officer tells him that while he suspected Campbell was a spy he did nothing about his suspicions, " 'because you could never have served the enemy as well as you served us,' he said. 'I realized that almost all the ideas that I hold now, that make me unashamed of anything I may have felt or done as a Nazi came not from Hitler, not from Goebbels, not from Himmler—but from you.' He took my hand. 'You alone kept me from concluding that Germany had gone insane' " (pp. 80–81).

Vonnegut demonstrates his own ability to express uncritical love in his portrayal of Campbell. He does not make him a villain, although he makes us aware of Campbell's villainy. The book is in the form of a confession, and we realize that Campbell, who had been capable of great love for his wife, somehow lost proportion and actually became the thing he pretended to be. (Vonnegut warns against that particular danger in his preface to *Mother Night*.) But he was not an evil man; he lived in an insane world—where love seemed impossible and where he lost his wife, who was the only real recipient of his compassion—and he somehow went crazy along with his world, for "generally speaking, espionage offers each spy an opportunity to go crazy in a way he finds irresistible" (p. 140). The death of his conscience takes him further away from the ideal saving illusion of the cosmic cool than any other Vonnegut character. Campbell, unlike Adolph Eichmann, whom he meets and analyzes, is perfectly and entirely aware of the moral implications of his actions, and he is willing to accept the responsibility and the guilt for what he can no longer excuse as acts committed for the good of his country. His moral awareness comes too late, however—too late because he is already beyond caring. Through Campbell, Vonnegut tells us that the artist must be responsible to human beings, not to countries and causes. Campbell does become the cause of evil, and the title of the book—a quote from Goethe explained in the preface by Vonnegut who claims to be the editor of Campbell's confessions—does identify Campbell with Mephistopheles. His sin, he tells us clearly, is that he has been "a man who served evil too openly and good too secretly, the crime of his times." Vonnegut creates some unusual tensions in the reader's mixed sympathy for and condemnation of Campbell, and the result is that he forces the reader to question his own conscience for serving good too secretly, if not evil too openly.

Campbell achieves a certain detachment that allows him to view death without alarm, but that is the only characteristic of the cosmic cool he ever does achieve. That he was capable of the kind of love and compassion necessary for the ideal posture in Vonnegut's world is clear from his intense love for his wife and his ultimate recognition of responsibility. But Campbell's love is much too discriminate; his ideal is revealed in the play he always meant to write called *A Nation of Two,* about two people whose whole world is each other. Discriminate love is not proposed as bad in itself, but when a man always delimits his love within a very narrow boundary he becomes capable of the kind of discriminatory hate that went into Campbell's anti-semitic propaganda. With his wife dead and the significance of his actions clear to him, Campbell becomes a walking dead man; his con-

science is still alive and he has humility, but he is too
empty to give, to sympathize, or to have compassion. His
detachment comes not out of the desire to stay alive, but
out of a feeling that death could be no worse than life.
He has the sensibility to value the balance of the cosmic
cool, but has lost all chance of achieving it. His final
gesture is the diametric opposite of Eliot Rosewater's gesture—it is atrophy instead of expansion; it is the gesture
of a man who discovers he is entirely unable to live in
the world. It comes just after he has been formerly freed
of his war crimes, freed to be alone with himself again.

> So, I am about to be a free man again, to wander
> where I please.
> I find the prospect nauseating.
> I think that tonight is the night I will hang Howard
> W. Campbell, Jr., for crimes against himself.
> I *know* tonight is the night.
> They say that a hanging man hears gorgeous music.
> Too bad that I, like my father, unlike my musical
> mother, am tone-deaf. All the same, I hope that the
> tune I am about to hear is not Bing Crosby's "White
> Christmas."
> Goodbye, cruel world!
> *Auf Wiedersehen?* [p. 192, Vonnegut's italics.]

We might note that Campbell is unable to hear the
question asked in three other Vonnegut books—the "Poo-
tee-weet?" that Vonnegut associates with the balance of
the cosmic cool. Campbell's final question is much more
death oriented.

Vonnegut seems to identify himself closely with his
characters' confessions of guilt; we have already seen
that the connection between Vonnegut the narrator and
Billy Pilgrim in *Slaughterhouse-Five* reveals that Billy's

living death—a death of the spirit caused in large part by
his experience with the Dresden slaughter—is something
Vonnegut fears possible for himself. The Jr. in Howard
W. Campbell, Jr.'s name makes us wonder, in that case,
how much Kurt Vonnegut, Jr., identifies with Campbell's
confessions. In *Slaughterhouse-Five*, I believe, Vonnegut
purposely intrudes himself as a character appearing in
the first and last chapters of the book, surrounding the
story of Billy Pilgrim, in order to test his own personal
ability to achieve the posture of the cosmic cool. Billy
himself, as we have seen, *appears* both detached and compassionate enough to have achieved the ideal balance,
but it is all an appearance. He is really a man whose will
to live—never more than a precarious thing to begin
with—has been deadened by Dresden and by the harmful
illusion that all things are determined, that everything
has always happened and nothing can change. And this
is a harmful illusion, for while it allows Billy to exist
physically, it also allows him to be absolved from the
guilts of war without the cost of compassion. But Vonnegut the narrator believes man can still learn to be kind
and end wars—he believes he himself can still write an
antiwar novel where war is not glorified but labeled an
obscene "Children's Crusade." Yet he does fear that the
same detached perspective, the cosmic vantage point,
which helps him recognize man's pride and the necessity
for conscience and compassion could lead him to Billy
Pilgrim's kind of deadness. It could do that because it is
based on the memory of Dresden, which not only demands some detachment but provides a constant temptation to give up and withdraw. The writing of *Slaughterhouse-Five*, however, is a special act of love for Vonnegut;
it is a fable, he tells us, he has been a long time trying
to write, a fable that exorcises his own terrors and guilts

and convinces him he is able to invent and therefore live and love under the illusion of the cosmic cool. "Sam—here's the book," he tells his publisher:

> It is so short and jumbled and jangled, Sam, because there is nothing intelligent to say about a massacre. Everybody is supposed to be dead, to never say anything or want anything ever again. Everything is supposed to be very quiet after a massacre, and it always is, except for the birds.
>
> And what do the birds say? All there is to say about a massacre, things like *"Poo-tee-weet?"* [p. 17]

Vonnegut's fable proves that he is not dead, that—like T. S. Eliot's poet-prophets, also symbolized by birds—he can still say something, even if it is only the "Poo-tee-weet?" that symbolizes the illusion of the cosmic cool. Like Pynchon's Fausto Maijstral, he has glimpsed annihilation in Dresden and come back from his view of the dead. Vonnegut tells us Lot's wife was turned to a pillar of salt for looking back on the destruction of Sodom and Gomorrah. He tells us *Slaughterhouse-Five* is a failure because it was written by a pillar of salt who looked back on Dresden. But the truth is, it is a success on some levels: it is one way of dealing with historical fact—an intensely personal way and a way that seems to be very popular in the late sixties; it is a confessional exorcism and an act of love for both the author and his reader. In it Vonnegut creates a true fable of someone managing to live in the world, coping with the agonies of massacre and the confusions of fabulous fact—true because that someone is Vonnegut himself. He is the someone who is able to achieve the balance of the cosmic cool, combining humility, compassion, love, and conscience with a detached control of these virtues, and the will to go on living. And because that someone is himself, he further perfects the concept of the cosmic cool, adding what is much needed in our world of guilt and terror—the dignity of self-respect. He need not fear that he is the spiritually dead Billy Pilgrim, the guilty Howard W. Campbell, Jr., who serves good too quietly, or even the frantic Eliot Rosewater whose best act is still only symbolic.

"Poo-tee-weet?" the symbolic bird asks in the last line of *Slaughterhouse-Five,* and the nonsense words become especially moving because we are witnessing more than a black humorist's symbolic affirmation of life, and more than a fabulist's act of love—we are witnessing a moment of balance in Vonnegut's own life, when he finds himself capable of dealing with the intense pain of his Dresden experience and ready to go on with the delicate business of living.

The overall didactic tone of Vonnegut's work—the less personal tone—is not quite so hopeful as my last remarks would indicate. Cataclysm seems more possible than the cosmic cool, given Vonnegut's dark vision of man's inhumanity to man. The threat of cataclysm is made possible by certain sins men commit not because they are evil but because they are foolish and live by the wrong illusions, illusions that result in the loss of conscience. These pathetic sinners are Vonnegut's versions of the wastelander—he usually calls them "Hoosiers" of one sort or another. All of his characters whose pride threatens the world in some way are from Indianapolis or some other Indiana town, or they are from Illium, New York—code name for Schenectady. These are places with "lively native American fascists" where—as Vonnegut tells us when he describes Pisquontuit, Rhode Island, in one of the few times he briefly varies his locale—the lives led "were nearly all paltry, lacking in subtlety, wisdom, wit or invention—were precisely as pointless and unhappy as lives led in Rosewater, Indiana" (*GBMR,* p. 114). It is not the pathetic quality of their little lives that makes Vonnegut's Hoosiers into sinners—it is the immense uncaring self-centeredness of their pride, and Vonnegut seems to find the term useful as a label for anyone guilty of such pride. He makes his use of the term clear in *Cat's Cradle* where a couple of ugly Americans pounce on the narrator; the woman, wanting to be called "Mom," assures the narrator that as a Hoosier he is welcome to the world.

> "My God," she said, "are you a Hoosier?"
> I admitted I was.
> "I'm a Hoosier, too," she crowed. "Nobody has to be ashamed of being a Hoosier."
> "I'm not," I said. "I never knew anybody who was."
> "Hoosiers do all right. Lowe and I've been around the world twice, and everywhere we went we found Hoosiers in charge of everything."
> "That's reassuring." [p. 80]

Looking at the sins of the Hoosiers reveals the most didactic side of Vonnegut's work, for he tells us frankly that these sins make our world a waste land and may soon make it a ruin. They lead in one way or another to a loss of conscience and to dehumanization because they perpetuate the illusions that war, money, machines, science, and causes are more important than people. The chief sin of all is the sin of pride, the pride of purpose. Bokonon often points out that people commit atrocities in the name of God, claiming to have some inside information on God's real purposes. It is because of the pride of purpose that one country wages war against another, destroying people for the sake of political or ideological ambitions. All wars, Vonnegut informs us in *Slaughterhouse-Five,* should be identified with the Children's Crusades, for they exist in one way or another because of the illusion of sacred cause, and they kill children—not men as John Wayne would have us believe—in the name of that cause. The futility and brutality of war takes a center spot in all of Vonnegut's work, and specifically the part war plays in dehumanizing people. He does not deny that wars have been sometimes necessary, but he sees them as sins nonetheless, for the sin of pride and the sin of war combine to produce what is undeniably the greatest threat of cataclysm. (Witness, for example, Senator Richard Russell's words spoken in the Senate in 1969: "If we have to start over with Adam and Eve, I want them to be Americans; and I want them on this continent and not in Europe.") Thus, the dehumanized Howard W. Campbell, Jr., in a last burst of feeling and passion, makes a simple and straightforward speech on these sins:

> "There are plenty of good reasons for fighting," I said, "but no good reason ever to hate without reservation, to imagine that God Almighty Himself hates with you, too. Where's evil? It's that large part of every man that wants to hate without limit, that wants to hate with God on its side. It's that part of every man that finds all kinds of ugliness so attractive.
>
> "It's that part of an imbecile," I said, "that punishes, and vilifies and makes war gladly." [*MN,* p. 181]

The sin of war also produces the illusion that death can be glorious, and that revenge is sometimes manly, moral, and justified. When the narrator in *Slaughterhouse-Five* tells people about his experience in Dresden, he invariably gets into this kind of situation:

I happened to tell a University of Chicago professor at a cocktail party about the raid as I had seen it, about the book I would write. He was a member of a thing called The Committee on Social Thought. And he told me about the concentration camps, and about how the Germans had made soap and candles out of the fat of dead Jews and so on.

All I could say was, "I know, I know. I *know.*" [p. 9]

The kind of morality that trades slaughter for slaughter ultimately leads to justification of Dresden and to a tricky sense of righteous revenge, pointed out by Vonnegut through his inclusion in *Slaughterhouse-Five* of Harry Truman's announcement that an atom bomb had been dropped on Hiroshima—a document which, despite any truly good arguments for historical necessity, demonstrates a certain pride in man's ability to obliterate anybody who "deserves" it. The honestly bewildering dilemmas involved in decisions like Truman's and in defending the morality of World War II make Vonnegut's point all the more valid, for these dilemmas ultimately make it easier to find just and good causes for total cataclysm. As the narrator in *Cat's Cradle* is told when he begins to glorify the way men die, referring to some deaths that occurred in the cataclysm that ends that book, "Well, maybe you can find some neat way to die, too."

In *God Bless You, Mr. Rosewater* Vonnegut deals with the sin of politics which creates such illusions as Free Enterprise and Human Productivity. Vonnegut stresses that politics can be sinful when it leads to ideas on how to discard useless people in favor of useful things. Senator Rosewater, an archetypal conservative politician, is one of the least human of Vonnegut's characters. He is a man who reduces life in America to two alternatives: "We can write morals into law, and enforce those morals harshly, or we can return to a true Free Enterprise System which has the sink-or-swim justice of Caesar Augustus built into it" (p. 37). When his son Eliot becomes ill from the immense exertions of his attempt to love useless and unneeded people, Senator Rosewater demonstrates how the political abstractions he preaches have unfit him for comprehending human problems and loving human beings. "This is basically a booze problem," he tells us, "If Eliot's booze were shut off, his compassion for the maggots in the slime on the bottom of the human garbage pail would vanish" (p. 59).

Other illusions indirectly connected to the sin of politics are the illusion of the value of money and the illusion of the natural superiority of the rich—both are stressed particularly in *God Bless You, Mr. Rosewater.* Both are illusions that lead away from compassion and conscience, and toward other sins—like greed and selfishness. There are also the sins of irresponsibility and schizophrenia—"the willful doing without certain obvious pieces of information"—and the sin of science which substitutes abstractions like Truth for conscience and Research for compassion. Felix Hoenikker, the father of the atom bomb and inventor of *ice-nine* in *Cat's Cradle* is the perfect portrait of the stereotyped scientist, totally ignorant of morality: Hoenikker, in his "childlike" little way, has to ask what sin is when it is mentioned to him in connection with the destructive potential of the atom bomb. The blanket sin for these several forms of moral blight might be called the sin of shortsightedness. Combined with pride and war, shortsightedness fosters all the illusions necessary for ultimate cataclysm. As the narrator of *Cat's Cradle* ponders: " 'What hope can there be for mankind,' I thought, 'when there are such men as Felix Hoenikker to give such playthings as *ice-nine* to such shortsighted children as almost all men and women are?' " (p. 199).

The moral to Vonnegut's tales is almost always a plea for uncritical love and compassion, but there can be sins of misused love when people like Billy Pilgrim's daughter in *Slaughterhouse-Five* find it very exciting to take someone's dignity away in the name of love. Abusers of love can be like the narrator in *Cat's Cradle* who, at first, wants to own Mona Monzano rather than share with her; or Amanita Buntline in *God Bless You, Mr. Rosewater,* whose name—a man eater—identifies her as one of a small number of women in Vonnegut's work who destroy human dignity on a small nagging scale. But if we were to compile a list of all the minor characters in Vonnegut's work, we would find, surprisingly, that there are as many good guys as Hoosiers. Although very few approach the posture of the cosmic cool, many do see the sin of certain illusions and the possible value of love. The morals in Vonnegut's fables are no more Meaningful and True than are the sins, but they do make life possible and maybe even a little more pleasant. These morals are usually stated flatly and without disguise, as one would expect from openly didactic fables. They might be summed up in one basic blessing—a blessing expressed by Eliot Rosewater as a baptism for newborn children and by Vonnegut as a baptism for the rebirth of his readers into some world a little beyond the waste land:

Hello, babies. Welcome to Earth. It's hot in the summer and cold in the winter. It's round and wet and crowded. At the outset, babies, you've got about a hundred years here. There's only one rule that I know of, babies—:

God damn it, you've got to be kind. [*GBMR,* p. 110]

"Would you call this age a good one for unicorns?" asks
a hunter in Peter S. Beagle's marvelous fable *The Last
Unicorn.* Considering the dreams of annihilation and
cataclysm that haunt the world pictured by the novel of
the sixties, we would not expect to find the fragile beauty
or crystal thin tenderness that is necessary for unicorns
to thrive. But Beagle provides these conditions and not
only is his book extraordinarily credible—which is a
marvel by itself in our time of measured cyncism—it is an
expression of much that is implicit, or perhaps muted, in
the novels we have already discussed. It is, in a sense, a
culmination of what the fable form contributes to the
novelist's vision of the sixties. As we have seen, all of the
novelists who have worried over our dreams of doom
have also fiercely defended life against death; they have
decried the world's weariness because they themselves are
not weary, but anxious to live. By shaping their visions
to fit the fable form, they have not just produced the
comic contrasts and tensions of the black humorist, they
have implied that there is a real wonder about human
life which needs to be incorporated along with the dark
fears of impending doom. The fable form provides them

with a way to intimate the value of life and the sense of wonder even while their content mourns the content of contemporary living. The juxtaposition of a bleak vision with a sense of wonder is briefly illustrated by one of Kurt Vonnegut's good guys, who tells us, "As stupid and vicious as men are, this is a lovely day." [1] The statement could have come from Pynchon, Elkin, Heller, or Hawkes as well as from Vonnegut; it is a kind of verbal expression of the tension that is sought in the black humorist's use of the fable.

Beagle takes this implied sense of wonder and makes it the central concern of his work. Wonder has been so obscured by the profusion of deadening detail in contemporary life that it takes a "pure" fable to retrieve it. There is no black humor in *The Last Unicorn* because form and content are unified to help us see again the small *happy* mysteries of human life and the magic of the world—if we dream dreams of annihilation, we do also dream some happy dreams. The fabulous mixture of fact and fiction in all the novels we have discussed so far should have prepared us to accept the wonder of unicorns and the possibilities of a qualified happy ending; *The Last Unicorn* not only celebrates what Pynchon and Vonnegut and others would like to openly celebrate, it restores a certain needed balance. The answer to the question of whether or not ours is an age for unicorns records Beagle's awareness of that need for balance: "No," says a second hunter, ours is probably not a good age, "but I wonder if any man before us ever thought his time a good time for unicorns." [2]

In a sense, Vonnegut and Beagle together present the

1. *Cat's Cradle,* p. 288.
2. *The Last Unicorn,* p. 6. Page numbers for all further citations will be included parenthetically in the text.

full range of alternatives offered by what I have repeatedly called the novelist's vision in the sixties. Vonnegut gives us a choice between cataclysm and a certain
balanced state of detached but compassionate caring.
Beagle gives us a recognition of life's pains and sorrows,
but only a symbolically ponderous threat of annihilation;
he emphasizes, instead, the balance of caring and loving
with a world of wonder. Vonnegut prepares us to understand that a move beyond the waste land could as well be
a move toward destruction as a move toward rebirth, but
for Beagle the move—although it acknowledges life's
recalcitrance and the dangers of the Red Bull—is out of
the waste land and into the magic of life, as in his first
novel, *A Fine and Private Place,* where the main character literally moves out of a cemetery to rejoin the living.
The difference between the two visions can be defined
somewhat by each author's approach to clichés and folksy
truisms. Both burrow into a cliché and upset its usual
tired perspective, but Vonnegut does it to expose the
horror that can be concealed in the ordinary, while
Beagle hopes to revalue what we have seen too often—to
revalue by making us see anew. The rediscovery of
wonder in the world may ultimately be the best our decade can offer as a substitute for a truly accepted mythology to move us out of the waste land. The sixties seem
ripe for such a rediscovery; Tolkien has been gobbled
up with a great deal of enthusiasm, and the atmosphere
of the late sixties in particular is filled with "flower
children" and lectures on the false values that lead us
to exist without wonder. Although we might expect it,
Beagle's lovely fable is not a parody—it assumes a willingness to value things fresh and fragile and not necessarily sophisticated. Such an assumption is a sign of
health. Not only does Beagle succeed, I believe, in un-

earthing our own enchantment with the world, but he does so with his eye constantly on what is vital to our age —and such a "relevant" rebirth for the reader is surely a portent that we *can* move beyond the waste land.

There is a difficulty in talking about a fable that attempts to convey the experience of wonder—a difficulty reviewers have been quick to crow about.[3] The delicacy of such an experience and the delicacy of Beagle's book can be blotted by the critic's cold pen point, if he presses too hard. No doubt this is true—and it is true of Shakespeare too—for there is no critical structure that can replace the experience of the book itself. That is old stuff. The unjustifiable impulse for a critic to say only that he is tuned in and appreciative is, however, stronger than usual with *The Last Unicorn,* because the experience it conveys is so strangely vital and so strangely unfamiliar to us. The problem is complicated by the brilliance of Beagle's allegorical structure. Usually in good allegory there is a tension between the ideological level that characters represent and the human attributes of the characters themselves. This tension is made more beguiling by Beagle because the more human he makes his characters, the more he paradoxically reinforces their ideological function—for the main message of the allegory is that there is magic in being human. I hope to discuss that magic, the terms of the allegory, and the experience of wonder without either shirking the critic's responsibility and joining a secret society of aficionados, or seriously undoing Beagle's spell.

The story of *The Last Unicorn* is the simple romance of a female unicorn's quest to release all other unicorns

3. See, for example, Benedict Kiely, "American Wandering Minstrel: Peter S. Beagle and *The Last Unicorn,*" *The Hollins Critic* 5, no. 2 (Apr. 1968): 1–12.

from the tyranny of the mysteriously powerful Red Bull. The unicorn is aided by Schmendrick the Magician, Molly Grue, and Prince Lír. The quest involves an ultimate confrontation with King Haggard, father of Lír and keeper of the Red Bull, and a final battle with the Bull itself. Before that confrontation the unicorn is turned into the lovely Lady Amalthea by Schmendrick, and as the Lady gradually forgets her immortal nature, she and Prince Lír fall in love. The ending is, of course, a victory over Haggard and the Red Bull, and the unicorn's return to her nonhuman form. It is a magnificent romance with a sweetly sorrowful happy ending.

The meanings of the allegorical figures are—as in most twentieth-century allegory—widely suggestive rather than single objective manifestations of absolute divine Truth. Each figure contributes to an overall image of what it is to be human, what it is to be an artist, and what it is to be alive in a world of wonder. The unicorn herself is a dream of beauty, the kind of dream that makes humans wake weeping with a sense of human loss, and the knowledge of unbearable beauty. The reader requires no special knowledge of the mythological unicorn to catch Beagle's creation—Beagle tells us no golden bridle is needed, nor any other apparatus; all you need is a "pure heart." The unicorn is the opposite of the dream of annihilation that dominates our lives according to Pynchon, Hawkes, and Vonnegut. She is the dream we have forgotten how to see, the thing whose absence makes our world a waste land; she is renewal and rebirth, the lost fertility and potency of life. When we learn to see the unicorn we will be healed and reborn and the world will be ripe again, as it is in the closing moments of the book. "She is a rarer creature than you dare to dream," Schmendrick tells us in a typical burst of lyrical but inept adoration. "She is a myth, a memory, a will-o'-the wish. Wail-o'-the wisp" (p. 51). Even when she is enchanted and turned into the Lady Amalthea, the unicorn's eyes "are full of green leaves, crowded with trees and streams and small animals." She is the embodiment of wonder and to be aware of her existence is to know the magic of the world, the silver underside of leaves. Just to have glimpsed her is enough to alter a man, like the Mayor's men who watch the unicorn disappear into the night "like a falling star," and who now and then after that "laughed with wonder in the middle of very serious events and so came to be considered frivolous sorts" (p. 55). Even King Haggard, the king of wastelanders, is touched with wonder when he sees the unicorn. In fact, he is always touched with wonder when he sees a unicorn, and for that reason he has used the evil power of the Red Bull to help him hoard all the unicorns and deprive the world of wonder, making it into the familiar wasted land.

Beagle uses the unicorn to help define what it is to be human. Because the unicorn is immortal she helps us understand time, death, and mortality. " 'It's the princesses who have no time,' " Molly Grue tells the unicorn. " 'The sky spins and drags everything along with it, princesses and magicians and poor Cully and all, but you stand still. You never see anything just once. I wish you could be a princess for a little while, or a flower, or a duck. Something that can't wait!' " And Molly adds in doleful verse:

> "Who has choices need not choose.
> We must, who have none.
> We can love but what we lose—
> What is gone is gone." [pp. 79–80]

The unicorn ponders for us, at random times, the human sorrow of growing old—the sense of loss, the pain, and the tears. When she does become a princess—the Lady Amalthea—and learns to love, we discover the value and beauty of man's fragile hold on time. Beagle seems to imply through the unicorn's shift from and to immortality, that love is made valuable precisely because we can *choose* it despite its inevitable brevity. The same thing is true concerning the magic of doing good—something Schmendrick discovers. Doing good, like love, cannot be valued for what it accomplishes, since the unicorn flatly declares, "You are a man, and men can do nothing that makes any difference" (p. 213). Loving and doing good must be chosen, as Lír and Schmendrick choose them, for the beauty and pleasure and wonder of loving and doing good. Otherwise, they are only swallowed up by time and never even achieve pleasure. This, of course, is the kind of universal concept usually explored by poetry, and it contributes, along with Beagle's style which often breaks into unannounced and sometimes comic verse, to the novel's lyric impact. The poetic conclusion in both *The Last Unicorn* and *A Fine and Private Place* decidedly includes the information that immortality is not so much fun—not even as much fun as mortality.

The paradoxes of sad pleasure and mortal love are only two of the many paradoxes about man that the unicorn exposes when she moves from unicorn to woman and back again. Man inspires simultaneous "tenderness and terror," and he, unlike a unicorn, is capable of "cruelty and kindness." When the unicorn is first changed to a human: "her face was the silly, bewildered face of a joker's victim. And yet she could make no move that was not beautiful. Her trapped terror was more lovely than any joy that Molly had ever seen, and that was the most terrible thing about it" (pp. 109–10). This image conveys something of Beagle's overall idea of what it is to be human. Not only must the unicorn be a "joker's victim" to be human, she must learn despair and weariness and pride, and yet she will still be somehow beautiful. Schmendrick has the final word on what it means to be human. "You can love and fear, and forbid things to be what they are, and overact" (p. 185). The combination of poetic paradoxes revealed by the unicorn adds up to Beagle's vision of the wonder of being human—the wonder and the pain.

The Red Bull, opponent of the unicorn, is Beagle's version of that same power or force we have seen continually in the novel of the sixties, the power that usurps man's control of his own life. The unicorn fears the Red Bull not because it seeks her death, but because it seeks to possess her very being. Fear and the Bull are constantly and closely identified—since it never fights, but only conquers, the Bull operates and succeeds only through the agency of fear. It unfits its opponents, turns them docile—as with the unicorns already captured and imprisoned in the sea—and leads them to the brink of annihilation. The Bull is immense, shapeless, and blind as fear; he drools thunder and "he was the color of blood, not the springing blood of the heart but the blood that stirs under an old wound that never really healed" (p. 100). He is "raging ignorance" and "a swirling darkness, the red darkness you see when you close your eyes in pain." It is the fear itself, and not the possibility of destruction, which Beagle insists conquers unicorns and makes the world a waste land—fear is always as big and as aggressively threatening as a Bull. There is no limit to the size of the Red Bull, and it seems to expand as its victim's fear expands. Beagle, in most of his imagery,

connects the Red Bull with sickness—with unhealed
wounds and pain—for the Bull must be eliminated to
heal the kingdom, to restore unicorns and the wonder
and fertility of life.

The Red Bull is very like the image of the wolf in
Who's Afraid of Virginia Woolf?—the archetypal image
of the ambiguous and unknown force that has gained
control of man's life. Beagle, too, does not really identify
that force; it does have something to do with fear, but
the threat is left to hover, combining the unrealness of
a cartoon and the mythical voraciousness of a wolf—
the mythical might of a bull—in an image of that unseen
force with its power vested nowhere that haunts us from
behind the facts of our daily life. The power could be
the Big Bad Bull as easily as it could be a Conspiracy or
an Institution, the sources of potentially demonic power
made specifically culpable by many novelists in the sixties. In any case, the Red Bull is the waste land maker,
and like Eliot's waste land, the Red Bull can never be
eliminated. When it does not vanquish, it vanishes, and
the wonder and fertility of the world are restored; but
the Red Bull never dies. To move beyond the waste land
the conquerors of the Red Bull must constantly renew
their victory.

King Haggard is the ostensible keeper of the Red Bull
—the Red Bull tentatively serves him as it would serve
others who were without fears because they were without compassion or hope. Haggard is the authority figure
who uses fear and the Red Bull to oppress his people and
keep his world a waste land. He is driven by greed and
selfishness to make a private possession of unicorns, and
thereby deprive the world of wonder. But Haggard is
not really an allegorical poke at authority; he is too sad
and too much without hope. He is, rather, the man who

prides himself on having no illusions and who loses his "heart's desire in the having of it." We are told that Haggard, speaking of food, repeats the old housewife's complaint with a new twist: " 'He says that no meal is good enough to justify all the money and effort wasted in preparing it. "It is an illusion," says he, "and an expense. Live as I do, undeceived" ' " (p. 140). Not only is such an anti-illusion attitude an enemy to wonder, especially the wonder of art, but it reveals a man who detests the sources of his own being. He sustains himself without delusion, and that could lead to sustaining himself without food. He has already destroyed his spiritual food, for while he genuinely does get pleasure from unicorns, his imprisonment of them betrays the source of his pleasure. Poor Haggard just does not know how to be content. He is truly the king of the wastelanders, burying himself and fearing the April of the unicorn that could stir his dull roots with spring rain. But he is particularly, paradoxically human because he wants pleasure even as he destroys it, and denies himself to prove that there is no pleasure. "His eyes were the same color as the horns of the Red Bull." He is weary of life, but anxious to exist, and tired and haggard from the emptiness of existence.

The sad side of Haggard makes him a tentatively suggested everyman: he is not so much the man to be beaten as the wound to be healed in all of us—the cure, of course, is the wonder of the unicorn and the human magic of love. The fragility of time does not lead Haggard to see love's value as others do; on the contrary, he tells us, "I always knew that nothing was worth the investment of my heart, because nothing lasts, and I was right, and so I was always old" (p. 164). Nonetheless, it is just precisely that haggard part of us which ultimately

reveals its own anathema—just as king Haggard does and
is wont to do—for nothing weary or hopeless can exist
if we are touched by the wonder of the unicorn, and
Haggard is unicorn-touched: "Each time I see my unicorns," Haggard confesses, "it is like that morning in the
woods, and I am truly young in spite of myself, and
anything can happen in a world that holds such beauty"
(pp. 164–65). Although they cannot heal Haggard, wonder and beauty can heal the rest of us as the unicorn
once "healed a king whose poisoned wound would not
close." The poison wound is our own haggardness, and
that is healed as King Haggard is destroyed—when the
unicorns are returned to the world, and our ability to
see them is restored.

One of the three aides who help the unicorn is
Schmendrick the Magician. Schmendrick, a kind of bum-
bling Prospero, an inept artist, has a tender heart but
is a doubtful craftsman. "I am Schmendrick the Magician," he announces in his more confident moments, "the
last of the red-hot swamis, and I am older than I look"
(p. 75). His ineptitude is so monumental that his teacher,
a famous wizard, felt sure Schmendrick was meant for
big things and so cast a spell on his life: "You shall not
age from this day forth, but will travel the world round
and round, eternally inefficient, until at last you come
to yourself and know what you are" (p. 113). To know
what he is as an artist is, of course, to know what place
magical wonder has in the world of the imagination—
when Schmendrick is cured of his ineptitude and his
immortality it is because the unicorns have returned to
the world. A world without wonder is a world where an
artist can be nothing but inept, so in order to know
himself, Schmendrick learns to value the fragility and
pleasure of beauty itself. Only in a waste land is there

no function for an artist, since there is neither beauty nor wonder; thus, the artist—as Eliot also pointed out—is unheeded and unneeded, for all he can do is make wastelanders feel uncomfortable. Schmendrick, at first, does not even do that: instead of producing a work of magical art, he "made an entire sow out of a sow's ear; turned a sermon into a stone, a glass of water into a handful of water, a five of spades into a twelve of spades, and a rabbit into a goldfish that drowned" (p. 33). When he does produce his first work of art, it is really a bit of plagiarism, for he evokes the presence of Robin Hood and his Merry Men.

But even when he performs the magical transformation of the unicorn into a woman, Schmendrick is not an artist in control of his craft—he tells us that the magic took possession of him; it was the art that chose, not the artist. As we have seen, however, a good human being learns to *choose* love for no other reason than its wonder; similarly Schmendrick learns that a good artist chooses to perform good magic under his *own control* because good magic is a very nice activity among the things a man can do with his little moment of life.

Before Schmendrick becomes a true artist he is troubled by the practical value of his art. He wants magic to be useful. In a waste land where the peasants are oppressed by King Haggard, where the unicorns are kept captive, and where greed, selfishness, and fear—as appear in Haggard and the people of Hagsgate—feed the brutal power of the Red Bull, an artist would like to feel relevant. He would like to do some concrete good. Schmendrick feels frustrated by his failure to be effectual in combating certain reactionary, anti-unicorn forces, and he is often reduced to shouting at wastelanders and conjuring good imaginative threats—like letters in the

Times: "You pile of stones, you waste, you desolation,"
he shouts at someone who is a menace to unicorns, "I'll
stuff you with misery till it comes out of your eyes. I'll
change your heart into green grass, and all you love to
sheep. I'll turn you into a bad poet with dreams. I'll set
all your toenails growing inward. You mess with me" (p.
39). Wanting to be useful leads Schmendrick to the brink
of despair and when the final encounter with the Red
Bull begins, he is willing to abandon the artist's quest,
a quest to find the value of magic and wonder. Before
he even attempts the supreme act of art—turning Lady
Amalthea back into a unicorn, or perhaps we could say
turning all humans back toward the rediscovery and rebirth of wonder—before he even tries, he despairs, for
he is not sure that such an act has value. "Let it end
here then, let the quest end," he says, echoing what has
been the eternal lament of any artist confronting his
times. "Is the world any the worse for losing the unicorns,
and would it be any better if they were running free
again? One good woman more in the world is worth
every single unicorn gone" (p. 185). It is the very same
problem that has influenced literary directions in the
past, and will probably be unusually influential on the
direction of the novel in the seventies. Its corollary asks:
is it not more human to give some concrete aid to the
sufferers of life than to write the greatest poem?

Schmendrick solves the dilemma when he realizes that
magic and art exist only for and because of the human—
in fact, the assumption of his powers, the making of his
magic as an artist, the end of his curse, and the discovery
of himself all come not because of any act of social char-
ity, but because in watching Lír's heroic courage he
comes to understand the value and beauty of being human. "Wonder and love and great sorrow shook Schmen-

drick the Magician then, and came together inside him, and filled him, filled him until he felt himself brimming and flowing with something that was none of these" (p. 191). Heroic courage, as we shall see, is for heroes; artists, according to the tale, are meant to forge something magically human from wonder, love, and sorrow. Schmendrick learns what we have learned: the fable is an act of love, and needs no other use. It exists so we can sing, as Schmendrick sings, *"I did not know that I was so empty, to be so full"* (p. 191, Beagle's italics). Man, as the unicorn points out, is not a meaningful creature and nothing he does will matter, but he can choose, nonetheless, to create and to understand that being human might mean living in a world of wonder. The choice will not restore Eliot's poet-prophet, or Prospero's brave new world, but Beagle maintains it can at least help us resee the world, and in that there might be a rebirth beyond the waste land, a rebirth for us all since we all can be filled with the wizard's wonder just by learning to see. "That is most of it," Schmendrick tells us, "being a wizard—seeing and listening. The rest is technique" (p. 168).

The inspiration for Schmendrick's discovery of himself and for the unicorn's success against the Red Bull comes from the hero of the tale, Prince Lír. The Prince's birth is attended by all the proper portents but he does not really hit his heroic stride until after he meets the Lady Amalthea and falls deeply in love with her. Then he courts her with all the usual claptrap of romance heroes.

I have swum four rivers, each in full flood and none less than a mile wide. I have climbed seven mountains never before climbed, slept three nights in the Marsh of the Hanged Man, and walked alive out of that forest

where the flowers burn your eyes and the nightingales
sing poison. I have ended my betrothal to the princess
I had agreed to marry—and if you don't think that
was a heroic deed, you don't know her mother. I have
vanquished fifteen black knights waiting by fifteen
fords in their black pavilion, challenging all who come
to cross. [pp. 131–32]

And the deeds go on, involving dragons and ogres and
one brother-in-law of an ogre. But none of this wins the
Lady Amalthea. Nothing does until she begins to forget
her immortal nature, and then she is won by a gentle
song, a little tenderness, and a pure heart. Lír, who is a
decidedly sweet hero, has to redo his theories of herohood, and he proves equal to the task. When he is
offered the choice between keeping the Lady Amalthea
for himself and allowing her to become a unicorn again,
his response is magnificent. He knows what his selfishness
could mean; if he repeats Haggard's folly he will deprive
the world of wonder and make it continue as an arid
waste land. "The true secret of being a hero," he tells
us from his unicorn-inspired vision, "lies in knowing the
order of things. . . . Things must happen when it is time
for them to happen. Quests may not simply be abandoned; prophecies may not be left to rot like unpicked
fruit; unicorns may go unrescued for a long time, but
not forever. The happy ending cannot come in the middle of the story" (p. 186). He cannot hoard the magic
that could heal the ailing waste land—he cannot, that is,
and still be a hero, and he must be a hero; Lír's sense of
decorum tells him that; it is why he is in the story. He
has, as he tells us, been reborn because of the unicorn—
he has come to see what it means to be human and to
see the value of living in a mortal's world. "You were

the one who taught me," he tells Lady Amalthea, "I never looked at you without seeing the sweetness of the way the world goes together, or without sorrow for its spoiling. I became a hero to serve you, and all that is like you. Also to find some way of starting a conversation" (p. 187). Through love Lír achieves the same vision of the world's wonder that Schmendrick achieves through his art and both discover the need for sharing. But Lír is called upon to perform an even more inspiring and truly heroic act than sharing his vision.

With the Lady Amalthea changed back to a unicorn, Lír, Schmendrick, and Molly Grue are forced to watch as the Red Bull drives the dispirited unicorn toward the sea. Lír is frantic with love and anxiety; he turns to Schmendrick, but the artist admits that wizardry is not much use in saving unicorns from fear—nothing is, in fact. Lír, however, will not accept such helplessness. "That is exactly what heroes are for," he says to Schmendrick, adding a touch of the active man's contempt for the poet. "Wizards make no difference, so they say nothing does, but heroes are meant to die for unicorns" (p. 195). With that he steps between the Red Bull and the unicorn. He is immediately crumpled and tossed to the beach; for, as we once learned from a secretive kitchen cat, it is a "valiant absurdity" to love a unicorn. Lír's gesture has no effect on the Red Bull, but the valiant *compassion* of his act penetrates the unicorn's fear, stops her flight, and she turns to defeat the Bull. Lír's heroism does not lie in any large dragon-sized deed; it comes from the simple and pure act of caring. Just as Lír has learned the love of wonder from the unicorn, the unicorn learns the wonder of love from Lír. Perishable as it is and foolish as it is, human love makes the unicorn envy the world of mortality. As in the Greek myths of old, we mortals know who has gotten the better hand from time's double-dealing. The unicorn, victorious but in sorrow "for the lost girl who could not be brought back," touches the battered Lír with her magic horn, lingering for the memory of love, and he is once again reborn. Lír is king now—king of a land restored to wonder and fertility as the unicorns have been restored to the world.

But you need not be a poet or a hero to comprehend the wonders of a unicorn-touched world. Molly Grue is neither—she is, in fact, a very ordinary everyday drudge like the rest of us, and she labors in her own way to aid the unicorn.

> Molly Grue cooked and laundered, scrubbed stone, mended armor and sharpened swords; she chopped wood, milled flour, groomed horses and cleaned their stalls, melted down stolen gold and silver for the king's coffers, and made bricks without straw. And in the evenings, before she went to bed, she usually read over Prince Lír's new poems to the Lady Amalthea, and praised them, and corrected the spelling. [p. 158]

She supplies the place of a sensitive lay reader for Schmendrick's art and Lír's romances, and she is confidante and confidence-builder for both men. She is also often Beagle's point of view for the reader. Specializing in neither art nor derring-do, she is still able to respond with tenderness to the value of the unicorn, and her response guides the reader. We are led to a layman's view of the world's wonder, and what better proof of the possibility of magic in the world than to be convinced of that possibility by poor, past-her-prime, not-very-special Molly Grue. Yet, even Molly does become special, and pretty, and loved, as she and Schmendrick end the tale by beginning a new quest to follow their unicorn forever, "a new journey, which took them in its time in and out of most of the folds of the sweet, wicked, wrinkled world, and so at last to their own strange and wonderful destiny" (p. 216).

It is a short step from the fabulous mixture of fact and fiction we have seen in many novels of the sixties to a traditional allegorical fable where the imagination is the only reality. But *The Last Unicorn* resists this kind of simplification. Beagle's allegory focuses on both the wonder of the imagination and the wonder of the world. There is some sort of thing we call a world that exists, in its mysterious way, outside the imagination. The artist, like Schmendrick, uses his illusions to explore the possibilities of the human imagination and ultimately to reveal the nicer magic in human life. The moral of the fable lies in learning how to see: good illusions, like the ones Schmendrick creates, lead to the discovery of unicorns; bad illusions like "Mommy Fortuna's Midnight Carnival" lead to dreams of annihilation—the same dreams Pynchon, Hawkes, and Vonnegut feared. We have already seen Schmendrick's good illusions, but there are other genres in Beagle's allegory of the imagination —there is, for example, the work of a marvelous butterfly who is not quite up to serious wizardry, but who has his popular appeal: " 'Death takes what man would keep,' said the butterfly, 'and leaves what man would lose. Blow, wind, and crack your cheeks. I warm my hands before the fire of life and get four-way relief' " (p. 11). And when asked if, as an artist of scraps and snatches, he can recognize who the unicorn is, the butterfly responds: " 'Excellent well, you're a fishmonger. You're my everything, you are my sunshine, you are old and gray and full of sleep, you're my pickle face, consumptive Mary Jane' " (p. 11). But the butterfly does understand what a unicorn

means, and even warns the last unicorn about the Red
Bull; gathering all his powers of concentration before
he departs to "take the A train," he sputters out: " 'No,
no, listen, don't listen to me, listen. You can find your
people if you are brave. They passed down all the roads
long ago, and the Red Bull ran close behind them and
covered their footprints. Let nothing you dismay, but
don't be half-safe' " (p. 13).

Most *humans,* however, are much more willing to see
the monsters in Mommy Fortuna's Midnight Carnival
than to see a unicorn. Mommy is the magician of evil
and ugly illusions, "bad fables" as they are called—
illusions that are inevitable when fortune becomes a
"mommy" who cackles at human willingness to believe
in nightmares. Her specialty is "stormy dreams sprung
from a grain of truth." People come to see her animals
and, as the unicorn points out, their willingness to believe in ugly things makes a poor unhappy dog into a
terrible Cerberus, or a plain crocodile into a fire-breath-
ing dragon. Bad illusions can even spoil the artist: take
the spider—in Mommy's carnival she becomes the
mythical Arachne, and, worst of all, she believes it. So
the illusions she spins are the most dangerous, because
"she sees those cat's-cradles herself and thinks them her
own work." They are cat's cradles like the ones pointed
out by Vonnegut or Pynchon that seduce us with the
glamorous prospect of our own annihilation—look at
her webs and your eyes go "back and forth and steadily
deeper, until they seem to be looking down into great
rifts in the world, black fissures that widened remorse-
lessly and yet would not fall into pieces as long as
Arachne's web held the world together" (p. 23). The
humans who come to the Carnival and almost all the
humans that the unicorn meets can see these unhappy

illusions, but they cannot see the unicorn. Because of the Red Bull, because of fear, they see nothing but the possibilities of death, and so the land is wasted and wonder, when it does appear, cannot be recognized. "I suppose I could understand it if men had simply forgotten unicorns," the unicorn reflects over man's surprising blindness, "or if they had changed so that they hated all unicorns now and tried to kill them when they saw them. But not to see them at all, to look at them and see something else—what do they look like to one another, then? What do trees look like to them, or houses, or real horses, or their own children?" (p. 10). Beagle's moral—if we need to call it that—is clear; we live in a waste land because we *choose* to look at death, and have either forgotten how to see the world's wonder or, having seen it, grow haggard in trying to possess it, thereby losing our heart's desire in the having of it. And if that is not the moral, then this statement from the unicorn must be—something to keep in mind when faced with harpies or red bulls—"You must never run from anything immortal. It attracts their attention."

The waste land imagery in *The Last Unicorn* is explicit—even down to crowning Lír's initiation as a hero with a sound described as the crowing of a cock. The whole last chapter describes the healing of the land after the return of the unicorns and the rebirth of Prince Lír. As a hero, Lír learns what we have seen consistently in the novel of the sixties—the heroic value of caring. It is the only weapon the individual seems to have against the overwhelming forces that haunt him in these novels. It is a weapon no bigger than the fable itself, and no bigger than the smallest act of love. Very likely, as I have mentioned before—particularly in the Introduction—the novelist of the seventies will not accept the move beyond

the waste land made by Beagle, Vonnegut, Elkin, Pynchon, and the others we have looked at. They may perhaps accept the will to move, the will to live, but it is
already becoming evident that they will have their own
vehicle of transportation. Writers who have lived with
the cold war and Vietnam instead of Dresden or Hiroshima, and writers who have experienced some affluence
and not the Depression are bound to have different responses: so too will those writers who have experienced
the ghetto, the false promise of freedom, and neighborly
oppression. In any case, if we can believe the portents
surrounding student involvement in politics, Black ac-
tivism, or the direction taken by Norman Mailer—who
always seems ahead of his times and behind his times all
at once—the fable and its contrived control of the outrageous facts of contemporary life may be found inadequate. Consider the following comments about Mailer's
Miami and the Siege of Chicago:

> Between the quiet inexorability of Miami and the
> porcine hysteria of Chicago, there seemed less and less
> room for aesthetic sportiveness, and, as the pressure of
> these events increased, one felt Mailer's constriction
> of spirit, a slow sentence-by-sentence admission that
> there are forces of obliteration uncovered by even the
> most intricate artifice.[4]

Aesthetic sportiveness and intricate artifice are exactly
what have distinguished the novels I have discussed—
they are what Pynchon, Vonnegut, and Beagle have used
to handle the forces of obliteration. The total loss of
such a response, although it may result in new ways to

4. Jack Richardson, "The Aesthetics of Norman Mailer," *New
York Review of Books*, 8 May 1969, p. 4.

move beyond the waste land, may very likely threaten a constriction of spirit.

On the other hand, the one major theme from the sixties that seems destined to be expanded in the coming years is the fear that some power has gained control over our lives. Black writers, like LeRoi Jones, have already relied heavily on this theme with the important difference that the obstacles to the individual's control over his own life—the obstacles to self-determination—are concrete and combatable for the Blacks. Thus a new vitality is possible, and certainly a new response, because the Black writer seems convinced that the individual's loss of control over his own life is not a necessary result of human nature and the irreversibly dehumanized modern world—it is, instead, a result of social conditions which could conceivably be changed. Paradoxically, this gives the Black writer a kind of hope that white writers discount more and more, the hope generated by a belief that certain decided actions may bring about liberation. No matter how remote the chance is, hope lies in the confidence that there is a way and the way is definable. This could mean a turning away from paranoia and it could mean the end of the passive hero—at least for awhile. The prospect is both exciting and frightening, for while we certainly do hope that the Blacks succeed in removing obstacles to freedom, we fear that—putting aside the happy social gains—the step beyond those obstacles would discover the same waste land we have seen, where *no* modern man—simply because he is modern man—is able to control his own life.

This, of course, is only speculation. In the meantime, I end my discussion of the novel in the sixties with Beagle's happy fable, an ending somewhat unrepresentative of the bulk of dark visions we have seen; but, then, what better way to end a discussion of the fable than with a happy ending? As Schmendrick the Magician would say:

"Haven't you ever been in a fairy tale before?"

SELECTED BIBLIOGRAPHY

(No attempt has been made to list the complete works of any author. Novels, interviews, and critical articles are listed as clearly as possible according to their relationship to the three part division of the book.)

GENERAL BACKGROUND

Chase, Richard. *The American Novel and Its Tradition.* New York: Doubleday, Anchor Books, 1957.

Eliot, T. S. "The Waste Land," from *Collected Poems: 1909–1935.* New York: Harcourt Brace, 1936.

James, Henry. *The Art of the Novel.* Edited by R. P. Blackmur. New York: Scribner paperback, 1934.

Lewis, R. W. B. *The American Adam.* Chicago: Univ. of Chicago Press, 1955.

Weston, Jessie L. *From Ritual to Romance.* Garden City, N.Y.: Doubleday, Anchor Books, 1957.

BACKGROUND ON THE CONTEMPORARY NOVEL

Aldridge, John W. *Time to Murder and Create.* New York: McKay, 1966.

Bier, Jesse. "Recent American Literature: The Great Debate." *Bucknell Review* 14 (May 1966): 98–105.

Bryant, Jerry H. *The Open Decision.* New York: Macmillan, Free Press, 1970. Although I have not yet had time to review this work, I include it here since it deals with the contemporary American novel.

Fiedler, Leslie. *The Return of the Vanishing American.* New York: Stein & Day, 1968. Also available in paperback from Stein & Day.

———. *Waiting for the End.* New York: Stein & Day, 1964. Also available in paperback from Stein & Day.

Fuller, Edmund. *Books with Men behind Them.* New York: Random House, 1962.

Gindin, James. "The Fable Begins to Break Down." *Wisconsin Studies in Contemporary Literature* 8 (Winter 1967): 1–27.

Gold, Herbert. "Fiction of the Sixties." *Atlantic* 206 (Sept. 1960): 53–57.

Greenberg, Alvin. "The Novel of Disintegration: Paradoxical Impossibility in Contemporary Fiction." *Wisconsin Studies in Contemporary Literature* 7 (Winter–Spring 1966): 103–24.

Hassan, Ihab. "The Avant-Garde: Which Way is Forward." *Nation,* 18 Nov. 1966, pp. 396–99.

———. "Beyond a Theory of Literature: Intimation of Apocalypse." *Comparative Literature Studies* 1 (1964): 261–71.

———. "The Dismemberment of Orpheus: Reflections on Modern Culture, Language, and Literature." *American Scholar* 32 (Summer 1963): 463–84.

———. "Laughter in the Dark: The New Voice in American Fiction." *American Scholar* 33 (Autumn 1964): 636–38, 640.

———. *Radical Innocence.* Princeton: Princeton Univ. Press, 1961. Also available in paperback from Harper & Row, Colophon Books.

———. "The Way Down and Out: Spiritual Deflection in Recent American Fiction." *Virginia Quarterly Review* 39 (Winter 1963): 81–93.

Hoffman, Daniel. *Form and Fable in American Fiction.* New York: Oxford Univ. Press, 1961. Also available in paperback from Oxford Univ. Press.

Kazin, Alfred. "The Alone Generation: A Comment on the Fiction of the 'Fifties." *Harper's* 209 (Oct. 1959): 127–31.

———. *Contemporaries.* Boston: Little, Brown, Atlantic Monthly Press, 1962.

Klein, Marcus. *After Alienation.* Cleveland: World Publishing Co., Meridian Books, 1962.

Levine, Paul. "The Intemperate Zone: The Climate of Contemporary American Fiction." *Massachusetts Review* 8 (Summer 1967): 505–23.

Littlejohn, David. "The Anti-Realist." *Daedalus* 92 (Spring 1963): 250–64.

Miller, James E., Jr. *Quests Surd and Absurd*. Chicago: Univ. of Chicago Press, 1967.

Moore, Henry T. "Campus in Wonderland." *CEA Critic* 23 (May 1961): 1, 8.

Roth, Philip. "Writing American Fiction." *Commentary* 31 (Mar. 1961): 223–33.

Rovit, Earl H. "American Literature and 'The American Experience.'" *American Quarterly* 13 (Summer 1961): 115–25.

Scholes, Robert. *The Fabulators*. New York: Oxford Univ. Press, 1967.

Shulman, Robert. "Myth, Mr. Eliot, and the Comic Novel." *Modern Fiction Studies* 12 (Winter 1966–67): 315–403.

Tanner, Tony. *City of Words*. New York: Harper & Row, 1971. Although I have not yet had time to review this work, I include it here since it deals with the contemporary American novel.

Whitbread, Thomas B., ed. *Seven Contemporary Authors*. Austin, Texas: Univ. of Texas Press, 1966.

PART I

Novels

Baker, Elliott. *A Fine Madness*. New York: Putnam, 1964. Also available in paperback from New American Library, Signet Books.

———. *The Penny Wars*. New York: Putnam, 1968. Also available in paperback from Simon & Schuster, Pocket Books.

Barth, John. *Giles Goat-Boy*. Garden City, N.Y.: Doubleday, 1966. Also available in paperback from Crest Fawcett World.

Boles, Robert. *The People One Knows*. Cambridge, Mass.: Houghton Mifflin, 1964.

Charyn, Jerome. *Going to Jerusalem*. New York: Viking Press, 1967.

———. *On the Darkening Green*. New York: McGraw-Hill, 1965.

Donohue, H. E. F. *The Higher Animals: A Romance.* New York: Viking Press, 1965.

Elkin, Stanley. *A Bad Man.* New York: Random House, 1967. Also available in paperback from Berkley, Medallion Press.

Fariña, Richard. *Been Down So Long It Looks Like Up to Me.* New York: Random House, 1966. Also available in paperback from Dell.

Heller, Joseph. *Catch-22.* New York: Simon & Schuster, 1961. Also available in paperback from Dell.

Kesey, Ken. *One Flew over the Cuckoo's Nest.* New York: Viking Press, 1962. Also available in paperback from Viking Press and New American Library, Signet Books.

———. *Sometimes a Great Notion.* New York: Viking Press, 1964. Also available in paperback from Bantam Books.

Kolb, Ken. *Getting Straight.* London: Chilton, 1967. Also available in paperback from Bantam Books.

Ludwig, Jack. *Confusions.* London: Secker & Warburg, 1963.

Midwood, Barton. *Bodkin.* New York: Random House, 1967.

Reed, Ishmael. *The Free-Lance Pallbearers.* New York: Doubleday, 1967. Also available in paperback from Bantam Books.

———. *Yellow Back Radio Broke-Down.* New York: Doubleday, 1969. Also available in paperback from Bantam Books.

Rogers, Thomas. *The Pursuit of Happiness.* New York: World Publishing Co., 1968. Also available in paperback from New American Library, Signet Books.

Spacks, Barry. *The Sophomore.* Englewood Cliffs, N.J.: Prentice-Hall, 1968. Also available in paperback from Crest Fawcett World.

Stegner, Page. *The Edge.* New York: Dial Press, 1967.

Wallant, Edward Lewis. *The Children at the Gate.* New York: Harcourt Brace Jovanovich, 1964. Also available in paperback from Popular Library.

———. *The Pawnbroker.* New York: Harcourt, Brace & World, 1961. Also available in paperback from Macfadden-Bartell Corp.

Yount, John. *Wolf at the Door.* New York: Random House, 1967.

Interviews

Enck, John J. "John Barth: An Interview." *Wisconsin Studies in Contemporary Literature* 6 (Winter–Spring 1965): 3–14.

Critical Articles

Barth, John. "The Literature of Exhaustion." *Atlantic* 220 (Aug. 1967): 29–34.
Critique, vol. 6, no. 2 (Fall 1963). The entire issue is devoted to John Barth and John Hawkes.
Doskow, Minnie. "The Night Journey in *Catch-22.*" *Twentieth Century Literature* 12 (Jan. 1967): 186–93.
Gordon, Caroline, and Richardson, Jeanne. "Flies in Their Eyes? A Note on Joseph Heller's *Catch-22.*" *Southern Review* 3 (Winter 1967): 96–105.
Henry, G. G. Mck. "Significant Corn: *Catch-22.*" *Melbourne Critical Review,* no. 9 (1966): 133–44.
Lehan, Richard, and Patch, Jerry. "*Catch-22*: The Making of a Novel." *Minnesota Review* 7 (1967): 238–44.
Lorch, Thomas. "The Novels of Edward Lewis Wallant." *Chicago Review* 19, no. 27 (1967): 78–91.
Noland, Richard W. "John Barth and the Novel of Comic Nihilism." *Wisconsin Studies in Contemporary Literature* 7 (Autumn 1966): 239–57.
O'Connell, Shaun. "Review of *A Bad Man.*" *Nation,* 27 Nov. 1967, p. 565.
Solomon, Jan. "The Structure of Joseph Heller's *Catch-22.*" *Critique* 9 (1967): 46–57.
Tanner, Tony. "The Hoax that Joke Bilked." *Partisan Review* 34 (Winter 1967): 102–09.
Waldemeir, Joseph J. "Two Novelists of the Absurd: Heller and Kesey." *Wisconsin Studies in Contemporary Literature* 5 (Autumn 1964): 192–204.

PART II

Novels

Berger, Thomas. *Reinhart in Love.* New York: R. W. Baron, 1962. Also available in paperback from New American Library, Signet Books.
Bourjaily, Vance. *The Man Who Knew Kennedy.* New York: Dial Press, 1967.

Constable, George. *The Imaginocrats.* New York: Harcourt Brace Jovanovich, 1968.

Donleavy, J. P. *A Singular Man.* Boston: Little, Brown, 1963. Also available in paperback from Dell.

Eklin, Stanley. *Boswell.* New York: Random House, 1964. Also available in paperback from Berkley, Medallion Press.

Ford, Jesse Hill. *The Liberation of Lord Byron Jones.* Boston: Little, Brown, Atlantic Monthly Press, 1965. Also available in paperback from New American Library, Signet Books.

Gass, William H. *Omensetter's Luck.* New York: New American Library, 1966. Also available in paperback from New American Library, Signet Books.

Hawkes, John. *The Lime Twig.* New York: New Directions, 1961. Also available in paperback from New Directions.

————. *The Second Skin.* New York: New Directions, 1964. Also available in paperback from New American Library, Signet Books.

Kelley, William Melvin. *dem.* Garden City, N.Y.: Doubleday, 1967. Also available in paperback from MacMillan, Collier Books.

Lieber, Joel. *Move!* New York: McKay, 1968. Also available in paperback from New American Library, Signet Books.

Neugeboren, Jay. *Big Man.* Cambridge, Mass.: Houghton Mifflin, 1966. Also available in paperback from Belmont Books.

————. *Listen Ruben Fontanez.* Boston: Houghton Mifflin, 1968.

Orlovitz, Gil. *Milkbottle H.* New York: Dell, Delta Books, 1968.

Percy, Walker. *The Last Gentleman.* New York: Farrar, Straus & Giroux, 1966. Also available in paperback from New American Library, Signet Books.

————. *The Moviegoer.* New York: Knopf, 1962. Also available in paperback from Farrar, Straus & Giroux, Noonday Press, and from Popular Library.

Price, Reynolds. *A Generous Man.* New York: Atheneum, 1966. Also available in paperback from New American Library, Signet Books.

————. *Love and Work.* New York: Atheneum, 1968.

Purdy, James. *Cabot Wright Begins.* New York: Farrar, Straus

& Giroux, 1964. Also available in paperback from Avon Books.

Pynchon, Thomas. *The Crying of Lot 49*. Philadelphia: Lippincott, 1966. Also available in paperback from Bantam Books.

———. *V*. Philadelphia: Lippincott, 1963. Also available in paperback from Bantam Books.

Rothberg, Abraham. *The Other Man's Shoes*. New York: Simon & Schuster, 1969. Also available in paperback from Avon Books.

Rovit, Earl. *The Player King*. New York: Harcourt Brace Jovanovich, 1965.

Sheed, Wilfrid. *Office Politics*. New York: Farrar, Straus & Giroux, 1966. Also available in paperback from Simon & Schuster, Pocket Books.

Shetzline, David. *DeFord*. New York: Random House, 1968.

Sontag, Susan. *Death Kit*. New York: Farrar, Straus & Giroux, 1967. Also available in paperback from New American Library, Signet Books.

Stone, Robert. *A Hall of Mirrors*. New York: Houghton Mifflin, 1966. Also available in paperback from Crest Fawcett World.

Sukenick, Richard. *Up*. New York: Dial Press, 1968. Also available in paperback from Dell, Delta Books.

Interviews

Hawkes, John. "Notes on the Wild Goose Chase." *Massachusetts Review* 3 (Summer 1962): 784–97.

———, and Graham, John. "John Hawkes on His Novels." *Massachusetts Review* 7 (Summer 1966): 449–61.

Critical Articles

Edenbaum, Robert I. "John Hawkes: *The Lime Twig* and Other Tenuous Horrors." *Massachusetts Review* 7 (Summer 1966): 462–75.

Frohock, W. M. "John Hawkes' Vision of Violence." *Southwest Review* 50 (Winter 1965): 69–79.

Hausdorff, Don. "Thomas Pynchon's Multiple Absurdities." *Wisconsin Studies in Contemporary Literature* 7 (Autumn 1966): 258–69.

Malin, Irving. *New American Gothic*. Carbondale, Ill.: Southern Illinois Univ. Press, 1962.

Maxwell, Robert. "Walker Percy's Fancy." *Minnesota Review* 7 (1967): 231–37.

Ratner, Marc. "The Constructed Vision: The Fiction of John Hawkes." *Studi Americani* 11 (1965): 345–67.

Rovit, Earl. "The Fiction of John Hawkes: An Introductory View." *Modern Fiction Studies* 11 (Summer 1964): 150–62.

PART III

Novels

Baker, Carlos. *The Land of Rumbelow*. New York: Scribner, 1963.

Barth, John. *The Sot-Weed Factor*. Garden City, N.Y.: Doubleday, 1960. Also available in paperback from Grossett & Dunlap, Universal Library.

Barthelme, Donald. *Snow White*. New York: Atheneum, 1967. Also available in paperback from Bantam Books.

Beagle, Peter S. *A Fine and Private Place*. New York: Ballantine Books paperback, 1960.

――――. *The Last Unicorn*. New York: Viking Press, 1968. Also available in paperback from Ballantine Books.

Berger, Thomas. *Killing Time*. London: Dial Press, 1967.

――――. *Little Big Man*. New York: Dial Press, 1964. Also available in paperback from Crest Fawcett World.

Blechman, Burt. *The Octopus Papers*. New York: Horizon Press, 1965.

――――. *Stations*. New York: Random House, 1964.

Brautigan, Richard. *In Watermelon Sugar*. New York: Four Seasons Foundation, 1968. Also available in paperback from Dell, Delta Books.

――――. *Trout Fishing in America*. New York: Four Seasons Foundation, 1967. Also available in paperback from Dell, Delta Books.

Coover, Robert. *The Universal Baseball Assoc., Inc.* New York: Random House, 1968. Also available in paperback from New American Library, Signet Books.

Demby, William. *The Catacombs*. New York: Random House, Pantheon Books, 1965. Also available in paperback from Harper & Row, Perennial Library.

Ely, David. *Seconds.* New York: Random House, Pantheon Books, 1963.

Fair, Ronald. *Many Thousand Gone: An American Fable.* New York: Harcourt Brace Jovanovich, 1965.

Feiffer, Jules. *harry, the rat with women.* New York: McGraw-Hill & Co., 1963.

Herlihy, James Leo. *Midnight Cowboy.* New York: Simon & Schuster, 1965. Also available in paperback from Dell Books.

Lieber, Joel. *How the Fishes Live.* New York: McKay, 1967.

Markson, David. *The Ballad of Dingus Magee.* Indianapolis, Ind.: Bobbs-Merrill, 1965.

Miller, Warren. *Looking for the General.* New York: McGraw-Hill & Co., 1964.

———. *The Siege of Harlem.* New York: McGraw-Hill & Co., 1964. Also available in paperback from Fawcett World Library, Premier Books.

Oates, Joyce Carol. *Expensive People.* New York: Vanguard Press, 1968. Also available in paperback from Crest Fawcett World.

Perutz, Kathrin. *Mother is a Country: A Popular Fantasy.* New York: Harcourt Brace Jovanovich, 1968.

Rovit, Earl. *A Far Cry.* New York: Harcourt Brace Jovanovich, 1967.

Southern, Terry. *The Magic Christian.* New York: Random House, 1960. Also available in paperback from Bantam Books.

Vonnegut, Kurt, Jr. *Cat's Cradle.* New York: Holt, Rinehart & Winston, 1963. Also available in paperback from Dell Books.

———. *God Bless You, Mr. Rosewater.* New York: Holt, Rinehart & Winston, 1965. Also available in paperback from Dell Books.

———. *Mother Night.* New York: Seymour Lawrence Dell, 1961. Also available in paperback from Avon Books. Reprinted in hardbound edition by Harper & Row, 1966.

———. *The Sirens of Titan.* New York: Houghton Mifflin, 1959. Also available in paperback from Dell Books.

———. *Slaughterhouse-Five or The Children's Crusade.* New York: Dell, Delacorte Press, 1969. Also available in paperback from Dell Books.

Interviews

Bryan, C. D. B. "Kurt Vonnegut, Head Bokononist." *New York Times Book Review,* 6 Apr. 1969, pp. 2, 25. Some comments made by Vonnegut in an interview are included in this article.

Critical Articles

Kiely, Benedict. "American Wandering Minstrel: Peter S. Beagle and *The Last Unicorn." The Hollins Critic* 5, no. 2 (Apr. 1968): 1–12.
Scholes, Robert. " 'Mithridates, he died old': Black Humor and Kurt Vonnegut, Jr." *The Hollins Critic* 3, no. 4 (Oct. 1966): 1–12.

INDEX